PERSEPOLIS
AND ITS SURROUNDINGS

HEIDEMARIE KOKH

PHOTOGRAPHS BY NADER DAII

Respected Ms. Corsini
I must thank you for providing me the opportunity to be in America which in return would favour the needy children caused by cancer.
I pray to god chrismas brings you & your family the wealthiest life in term of health & prosperity.
wish you a wonderful new year & god bless you.
[illegible]

For Ms Mary Corsini
with wishing health and happiness for her and those dear and near to her
warmest regards
Dan Palat
November 2008

YASSAVOLI
PUBLICATIONS

P E R S E P O L I S   A N D   I T S   S U R R O U N D I N G S

Koch, Heidemarie.	کخ، هایده ماری، ۱۹۴۳- م.
	(پرسپولیس اند ایتس سراندینگز).
Persepolis and its surroundings Heidemarie Koch; Photographs by Nader Daii.- Tehran: Yassavoli, 2006 = 1385.	
	۲۰۴ ص. : مصور، نقشه.
ISBN 964-306-293-7	انگلیسی
	فهرستنویسی بر اساس اطلاعات فیپا..
	۱. تخت جمشید. ۲. تخت جمشید -- آثار تاریخی. ۳.ایران --
Nader,	تاریخ -- هخامنشیان، ۵۵۸ - ۳۲۰ ق .م. الف. دایی، نادر
Perspolis and its surroundings.	Daii، عکاس. ب. عنوان:
۹۵۵/۶۳۲	DSR۲۰۷۹ /۵ک ۳خ
۸۳-۱۲۲۵۰م	کتابخانه ملی ایران

English Text: **Professor Heidemarie Koch**

Photographs: **Nader Daii**

Graphic Designer: **Aidin Avajeghi**

Bazaarcheh Ketab, Enqelab Ave., 13146, Tehran, Iran.

Tel.: (9821) 66461003 Fax: (9821) 66411913

80, Karim Khan Ave., Tehran, Iran.

Tel.: (9821) 88300415 Fax: (9821) 88832038

info@yassavoli.com

www.yassavoli.com

ISBN: 964-306-293-7

Pictures of pages : 35,68,75
belong to S.M. Aznaveh

IN THE NAME OF GOD

Historical Introduction

1.1. The Achaemenids

Until now it is uncertain where the Persians came from. They are Indo-European nomads who moved from central Asia to the south. They were first mentioned in records of a military campaign of the Assyrian king Salmanassar III in the year 843 BC. At that time they lived at the western shores of Lake Orumiyeh in today's Azerbaijan. The annals call these people Parsa ("Parsuvash"). This is the old Persian name for the people as well as for their country and their capital which the Greeks called Persepolis "city of the Persians". The word parsa has survived until today in the name of the Fars province.

Times were not at all safe in the region of Lake Orumiyeh in the 9th and 8th centuries BC. The Urartians in the north-west, the Medes in the east and south and above all the Assyrians in the south-west tried to gain sovereignty over the people bordering their country. Therefore the Persians moved further south where they came into the regions of the Elamite kingdom (fig. 1).

For thousands of years the Elamites had been eastern neighbours of Mesopotamia and its various inhabitants and - accordingly - most of the time in war with them. So the Elamites might have appreciated the strengthening of their forces by the arriving Persians during the uncertain times of the 8th c. In 691 BC, the Assyrian king Sanherib recorded that he had been confronted by the joined Elamite and Persian forces. And only a few years later, about 685 BC, the Persians owned fiefs all over the Elamite realm as we can learn from administrative tablets found in Susa. So, at that time, the Persians had reached those regions which became their homeland and from which they were to build up the first world empire in history.

The Elamite kingdom met its end after the total destruction of Susa by the Assyrians in 646 BC. Here and there, there were still confrontations with the Babylonian army, but the political situation remained obscure.

The eastern part of the Elamite territory with its capital Anzan (today Tall-e Malyan, 48 km west of Persepolis, see fig.1) must have been at that time already in the hands of the Achaemenid dynasty, because they called themselves "kings of Anzan". In 555 BC, the Persian Cyrus, who was later-on called "the Great", defeated the Median forces next to the fortress Pathrakata, in Greek sources Pasargadae. This was the end of the Median kingdom and the beginning of the Persian empire. Thereafter, Cyrus founded his capital exactly at this place. In 545 BC, after the victory over the Lydian king Croesus at the Halys River in Cappadocia he could add large parts of Asia Minor to his realm. This encounter is very famous because of the Pythian oracle of Delphi in Greece who had foretold Croesus: "If you go across the Halys River you will destroy a great empire" (Herodotus I 53). This river was the border between Lydia and Media. Croesus felt sure of his triumph and did not expect that his own empire was going to be destroyed.

In 539 BC, Babylon fell into the hands of Cyrus who thus annexed another important part of the near eastern world to his realm. But when he also tried to secure the north-eastern parts and campaigned in 530 against the Skythians across the River Jaxartes, today Syr-Darya in Uzbekistan, he was wounded and died. His follower was his elder son Cambyses while the younger Bardiya (Greek Smerdis) was put in charge of the satrapies of Parthia, Chorasmia, Carmania and Bactria. Cambyses' first deed was a campaign against Egypt which already his father Cyrus had had in mind. But, before Cambyses left he ordered his brother Bardiyato be murdered secretly, so that he could be sure that the latter wouldn't grab power while he himself was far away. The campaign against Egypt was a great success, Egypt together with Nubia were added to the Persian empire. But during Cambyses' absence a magus, that means a Median priest, with name Gaumata enthroned himself, pretending to be Bardiya, the younger brother of the king. Gaumata must have found out that Cambyses had his brother killed. Receiving those terrifying news Cambyses decided to return directly to Persia. But he never reached his homeland again because he died on the way.

Darius, a nephew of Cyrus, who had accompanied his cousin Cambyses as his spear-bearer to Egypt, decided to seize power, because there was no surviving male member of the family of Cyrus the Great. His first step was to get rid of the usurper Gaumata, who was very much liked by all the peoples of the empire because he had freed them from the taxes for three years. He had hidden himself in a castle in the neighbourhood of Pasargadae. There he was killed by Darius together with six helpers on September 29th, 522 BC.

This news spread very fast in the whole realm and in many places people revolted against the new ruler. Darius and his followers had to fight for one year in various regions of the empire. During this time they fought 19 battles and defeated 9 rebels who were called "lie-kings" by Darius. (see fig.3)

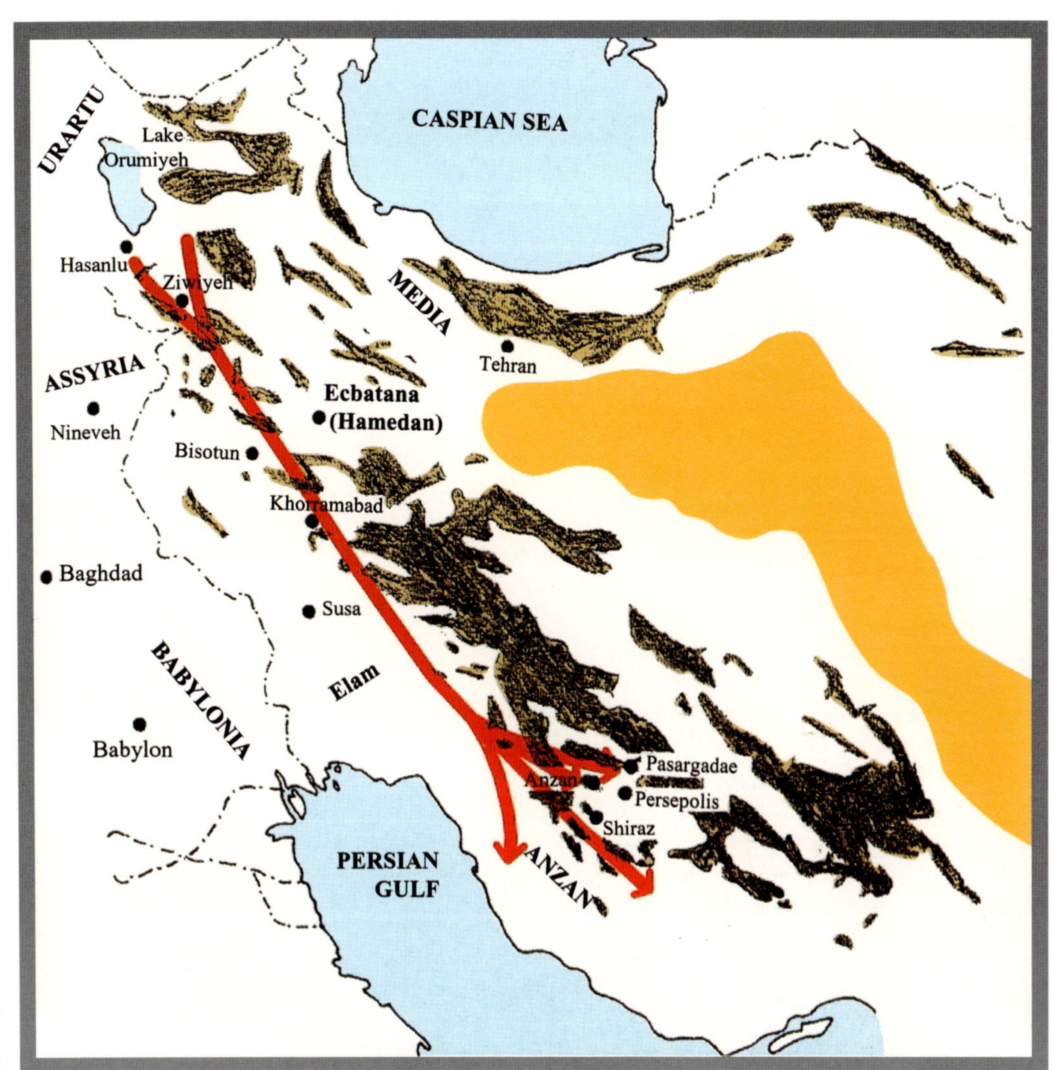

1 / The march of the Persians about 700 BC

On December 28th,521 BC the last battle was fought and Darius became real king of the great Persian empire. Under his reign it won its largest extension and reached from the Mediterranean Sea in the west to the Indus River in the east and from the Caspian Sea in the north to Egypt and Nubia in the south. Such an empire could be ruled only by a centralized and well organized administration. Examples of administrative clay tablets of the reign of Darius and his followers have been found in Persepolis, written in Elamite. Darius used the experience and knowledge of the Elamites who had developed an effective administration already in the 4th millennium.

During Darius' reign the empire remained more or less peaceful. The roads were secure and legations and traders travelled from one part of the country to another, equipped with travel documents for getting their rations in caravan stations along the road. In spite of this there were some revolts as, for instance, the Ionian rebellion in 494 BC. But, when Darius tried to subdue the Greeks his army was beaten in the famous battle at Marathon in Greece (490 BC). Also the attempt of his son and follower

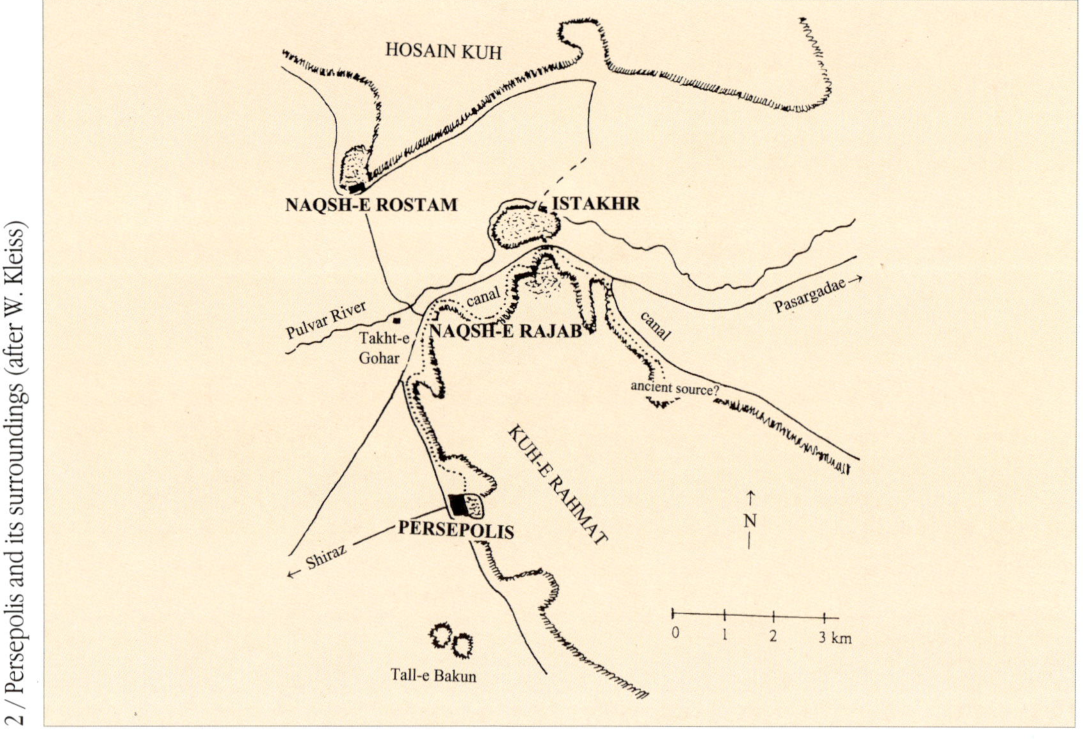

2 / Persepolis and its surroundings (after W. Kleiss)

Xerxes (486-465 BC) ten years later ended in a disaster and the loss of the fleet at Salamis. After this defeat Xerxes concentrated on the affairs in the centre of his empire and started immense building activities in the course of which he changed the whole appearance of the Terrace of Persepolis.
With the reign of Artaxerxes I (465-425/24 BC) the decline of the Persian empire started. Revolts not only in the provinces as Egypt and Asia Minor but also inside the royal family weakened the power. Princes killed each other and the question of succession to the throne was often solved with poison or iron. Alexander the Great (336/35-330 BC) overran the desolate kingdom with his army and became, after the decisive battles at Issos (autumn 333 BC) and Gaugamela (autumn 331 BC), the new ruler of the Persian Empire.
Alexander must have been very impressed by the high level of the Persian culture. He tried to combine east and west and married a Persian princess. Despite of this he could not prevent his soldiers from burning in the ecstasy of triumph the beautiful buildings on the Terrace of Persepolis, the capital of the Persian Empire.

3 / The triumphal relief of Darius the Great at Bisotun

1.2. Persepolis in the Post-Achaemenid and Sassanian Times

Alexander died very young in 330 BC. The Persian Empire was divided into the realm of the Seleucids in the western and northern parts and the Egyptian Ptolemies in the south. In the region of Persepolis itself a local dynasty remained, which is known only from their beautiful silver coins which were found there. Just one window frame has been preserved from the buildings of this time (see no. 5.2).

The Parthians, coming from the province of Parthia in the east of the Caspian Sea, succeeded in reconquering most parts of the Achaemenid empire under their rulers, the Arsacids, who claimed to be legal followers of the Achaemenids. During their long reign from the middle of the 3rd c. BC until they were defeated by the Sassanians in 224 AD, they were busy protecting their borders and themselves against the attacks from various sides. Well known are the wars against Roman armies. The capital of the Parthian empire was Ctesiphon in Mesopotamia. In Persepolis there are no traces of any Parthian presence. Quite different was the situation during the reign of the Sassanians. The ancestor of this dynasty, Sasan, was a local ruler and high priest of the Anahita sanctuary in Istakhr in the neighbourhood of the burial ground of the Achaemenid kings (see chapter 6 and 9, fig. 2).

4 / Statue of Darius the Great at the Archaeological Museum of Tehran

His grandson Ardeshir defeated the last Parthian king Artabanos V (213-224) in 224 AD. Two years later Ardeshir (middle-Persian form of Artaxerxes) was crowned in Ctesiphon a new king of the realm. His son Shapur I (241-272) was especially successful, enlarged the kingdom and beat the Roman army on several occasions. This is celebrated with large rock reliefs (see no. 7.3). From 38 known Sassanian rock reliefs 30 are in Fars. They were executed only during the reign of the early Sassanian kings.

5 / Detail of the triumphal relief of Darius the Great at Bisotun

1.3. The Rediscovery of Persepolis

In the middle of the 7th c. the Sassanian empire was defeated by Islamic armies. In the following centuries it more or less disappeared from the knowledge of the western world. Nobody knew about the activities of Islamic scholars and geographers exploring Iran. The crusaders were only interested in the "Holy Land" and not in countries lying further to the east. The first reliable descriptions of Persepolis reached Europe in the 16th c. under the reign of the Safavid kings. Travelling diplomats and traders were more and more attracted by the impressive ruins. Drawings were published, and especially the work of E.-N. Flandin and Coste roused admiration in the 19th c. The first photographs were taken for the large volume of Andreas and Stolze which came out in Berlin in 1882. But the first scientific investigations started only in the 20th c. Ernst Herzfeld conducted the first methodical investigations from 1931 to 1934. He was helped by the architect Friedrich Krefter whose skilful drawings revived the buildings of Persepolis. Several of them are illustrated in this book, too. After World War II E.-F. Schmidt continued the excavations in Persepolis and published the results in 3 large volumes. Last restoration works took place from 1964 into the seventies under the supervision of Iranian scholars and Italian architects, Ann Britt and Guiseppe Tilia.

Achaemenid Kings

Achaemenes
(ca. 705 - ca. 675 BC)

Teispes
(ca. 675 - 640 BC)

Cyrus I
(ca. 640 - ca. 600 BC)

Cambyses I
(ca. 600 - 559 BC)

Cyrus II
(559 - 530 BC)

Cambyses II
(530 - 522 BC)

Smerdis

Ariaramnes
(ca. 640 - 590 BC)

Arsames
(ca. 590-559 BC)

Hystaspes

Darius I
(522 - 486 BC)

Xerxes I
(486 - 465 BC)

Artaxerxes I
(465 - 425/4 BC)

Xerxes II
(425/4 BC)

Sogdianos
(425/4 BC)

Darius II
(425/4 - 405/4 BC)

Artaxerxes II
(405/4 - 359/8 BC)

Cyrus the Y.

Ostanes
(Artostes?)

Artaxerxes III
(359/8 - 338/7 BC)

Arsanes
(Arsames?)

Arses
(338/7 - 336/5 BC)

Darius III
(336/5 - 330 BC)

Early Sassanian Kings

Ardeshir I
(224-241)

Shapur I
(241-272)

Hormizd-Ardeshir
(272-273)

Bahram I
(273-276)

Bahram II
(276-293)

Bahram III
(293)

Narseh
(293-302)

Hormizd II
(302-309)

2. The Old-Persian Script

Many monuments in Persepolis bear inscriptions in cuneiform script. The Old Persian script was invented by order of Darius the Great (522-486 BC). This script was used for the first time on the relief in Bisotun, near Kermanshah on the old route leading from Babylon to Media, which was made to remember the triumph of Darius (fig. 3). The relief shows Darius accompanied by his bow-bearer and his spear-bearer. Darius sets his foot on a man lying at his feet and stretching his arms upwards for mercy. This is the image of the magus Gaumata. Nine "kings of lie" with their hands fettled on the back and tied with a rope around their necks step towards the king. At first Darius planned only this relief with a short inscription above his head. But this inscription was written in Elamite, because the Persians did not have a script of their own at that time. And also when the king decided to add an account to the relief for people in later times to remember his glorious deeds, this first account - to the right of the relief - was written in Elamite.

Then, he added a translation in Babylonian to the left. And then, he must have decided to create his own script for the Persians. The Persian version was added below the relief and in this inscription king Darius explicitly declared that this was a new script, that is, Aryan. The Persians called themselves Aryans, which means "noble, free".

This newly invented script is much easier than the Elamite or Babylonian script which were developing over 3000 years. And in addition to the old scripts the Persian script uses single diagonal signs to mark divisions between words. So in 1802, G.F. Grotefend in Göttingen in Germany was able to identify the first Persian signs, while H.C. Rawlinson did - independently from him - the same in England. These were first steps in deciphering cuneiform script.

And since Darius had written the same inscriptions in Elamite and Babylonian too, also the signs of the other cuneiform inscriptions could be read. Therefore, the monument of Bisotun is not only important for its historical value but also for deciphering cuneiform scripts in general.

The custom to write all his inscriptions in three languages, namely Old Persian, Elamite and Babylonian was kept by Darius on all his monuments. Therefore, three fields with different signs are always to be seen.

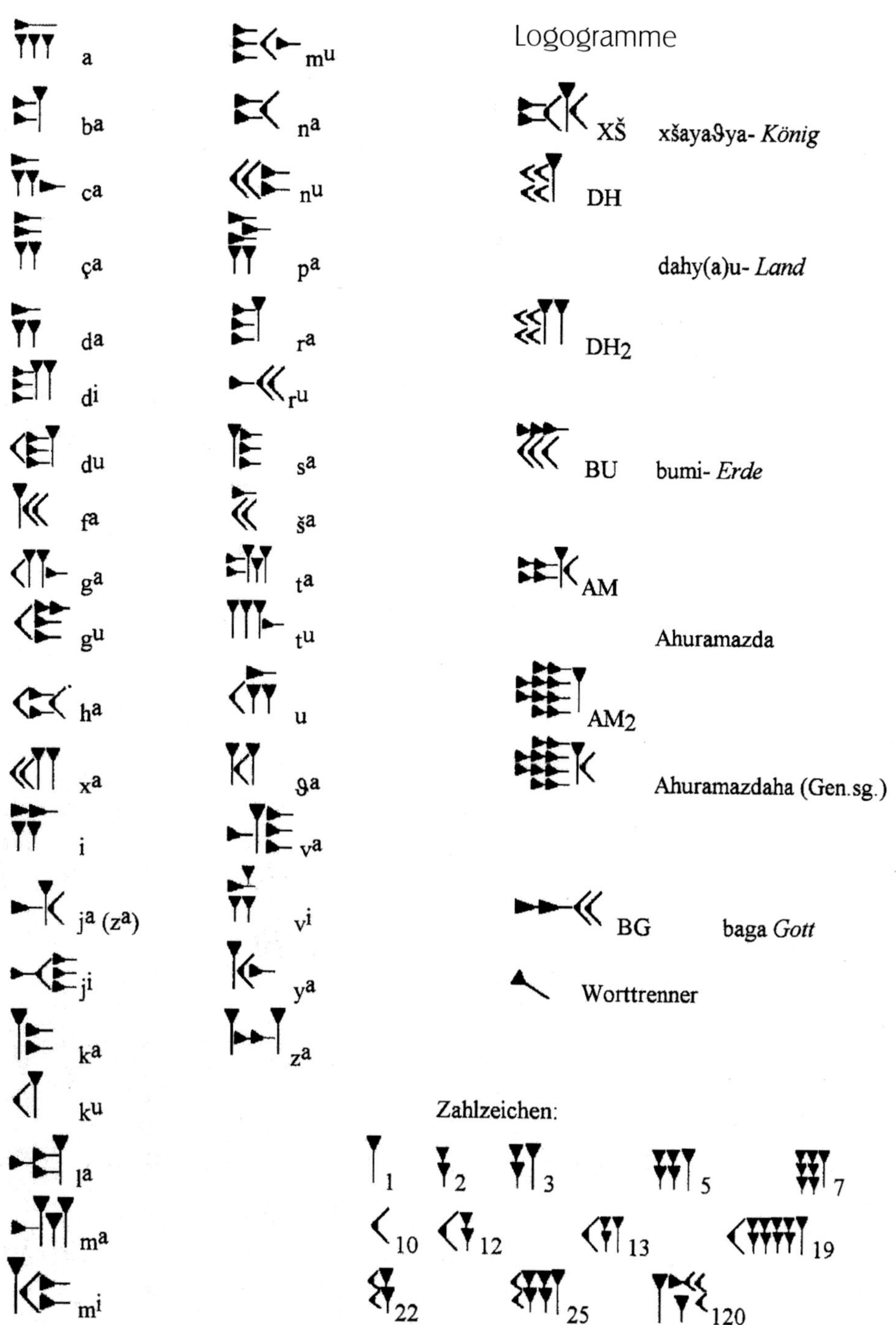
a
ba
ca
ça
da
di
du
fa
ga
gu
ha
xa
i
ja (za)
ji
ka
ku
la
ma
mi
mu
na
nu
pa
ra
ru
sa
ša
ta
tu
u
ϑa
va
vi
ya
za
Logogramme
XŠ xšayaϑya- König
DH
dahy(a)u- Land
DH2
BU bumi- Erde
AM
Ahuramazda
AM2
Ahuramazdaha (Gen.sg.)
BG baga Gott
Worttrenner
Zahlzeichen:
1
2
3
5
7
10
12
13
19
22
25
120

3. The Terrace of Persepolis - the Plan of King Darius

When Darius the Great (522-486 BC) had secured his power after crashing down all kinds of uprisings and revolts he first continued and finished buildings in Pasargadae which were begun by his uncle Cyrus the Great (555-530 BC, see chapter 10). Next he started to build a totally new palace in the capital of the old Elamite kingdom, in Susa, which was of high political importance. A palace built on such a place should impress his subjects and demonstrate the power of the new king. Therefore, it had to be a huge building, with stone columns, which was extremely unusual for that region, and lavishly adorned with all kinds of luxury which the Persian empire could provide. King Darius' dedicatory inscription (DSf) in which he describes in detail which materials were used and who were the people working together on this project has been preserved: "*The gold was brought from Sardis and from Bactria, which here was wrought. The precious stone lapis-lazuli and carnelian which was wrought here, this was brought from Sogdiana. The precious stone turquois, this was brought from Chorasmia, which was wrought here. Silver and ebony were brought from Egypt. The ornamentation with which the wall was adorned, that from Ionia was brought. Ivory which was wrought here, was brought from Ethiopia and from Sind and from Arachosia. The stone columns which were wrought here - a village by name Abiradush, in Elam - from there they were brought. The stone-cutters who wrought the stone, those were Ionians and Sardians. The goldsmiths who wrought the gold, those were Medes and Egyptians. The men who wrought wood, those were Sardians and Egyptians. The men who wrought the baked brick, those were Babylonians. The men who adorned the wall, those were Medes and Egyptians*".

This building was destroyed by fire and little is left to get an idea of its former splendour. But the description may help us to imagine more lively the former appearance of the buildings in Persepolis and their manufacture, too. Persepolis was a totally new creation of Darius the Great. In the heart of Parsa, the Persian mainland, and next to the place, where the last and decisive battle to ensure his power took place, he planned his residence as the centre of the empire and the symbol of his rule. On the slope of the mountain Kuh-e Rahmat, the "mountain of mercy", a huge terrace was built, 300 m wide and 455 m long. The bedrock could be only partly used while large parts were added in specially cut polygonal blocks of masonry. An impressive stone-wall, reaching 15 m high on the southern and western side, encloses the Terrace. At the top a great audience-palace was going

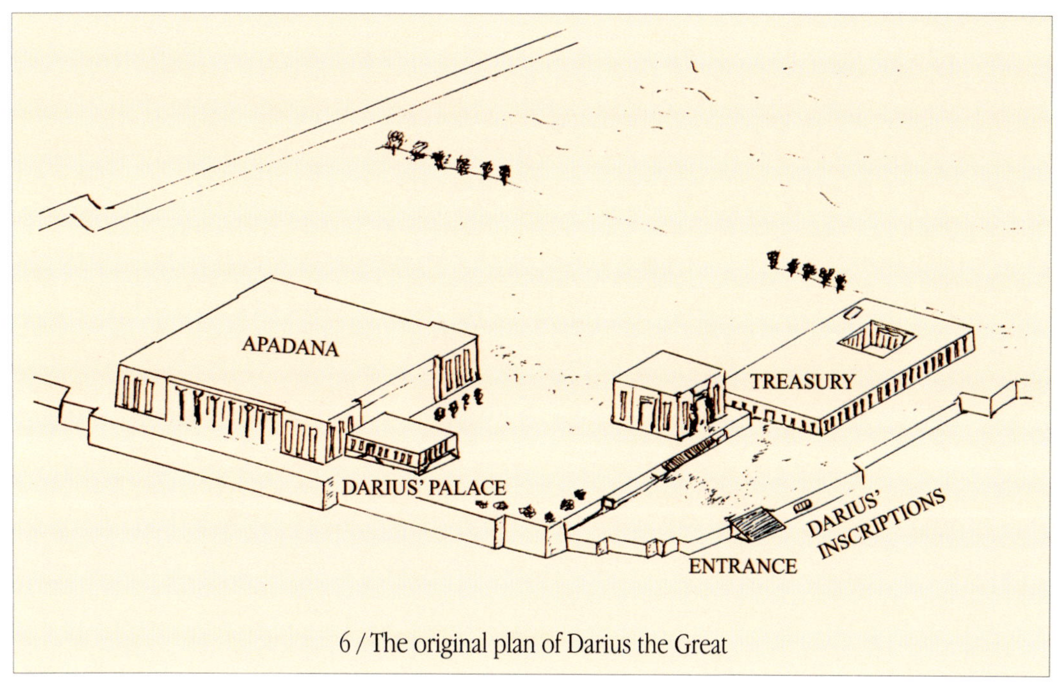

6 / The original plan of Darius the Great

to be built. Later sources reveal that such a reception-hall was called Apadana by the Persians. The Apadana was the most important building on the Terrace (fig. 6). Its place is more or less in the middle of the west side and directly above the wall. So it could be seen already from far away across the plain. Nothing disturbed this view because the first entrance to the Terrace was around the corner on the southern side. Here, a stairway led up to the Terrace and next to it Darius had a large inscription in Old Persian, Elamite and Babylonian carved into the walls. In the Elamite version the king emphasizes *"... in this place there hasn't been built a fortress before, according to the will of god Ahura Mazda I built this fortress, ... and I built it durable and beautiful and strong, so as I wanted it"*. This inscription could be read by every traveller who arrived at the foot of the Terrace and wanted to climb the stairs. After stepping up the visitor found himself on a large Terrace, from which the way led slightly upwards. Comparison with the earlier Achaemenid palaces in Pasargadae and Susa might suggest the existence of an entrance-gate. But no remains of such a gate are known. It may have been reused by Xerxes on another place (see no. 4.1). To the right hand the Treasury thick walls were made. Continuing further up the visitor saw to his left the facade of Darius' Palace facing him. And on the highest level of the Terrace the visitor was led to the east side of the Apadana, where a large space was left free for people to gather on special occasions. So, the east side was the main facade of the Apadana-building. It is, therefore, especially beautifully adorned with the most sophisticated columns, bearing capitals of lion-griffins, and the whole base is covered with friezes of reliefs. These reliefs reflect the function of the building. The king was seated in the middle, his crown-prince standing next to him (fig. 10 and 129-131); this relief is now to be seen in the treasury building, no. 4.14), receiving all the peoples of his empire. They are moving with their gifts towards him, while those who are backing up his power, the soldiers and the Persian dignitaries, are in his back (see detailed description of the building, no. 4.3). The reliefs reflect Darius' political program and show the importance of the building as a really imperial structure. The arriving visitor was immediately included into this program while he was guided in the same direction as the subject peoples on the reliefs and parallel to them he walked in the direction of the king who was expecting and receiving him.

When the idea of this program came into the king's mind or was proposed to him the building of the Apadana was already in progress. Because the Tilias, who were

7 / Reconstruction of the original plan of Darius the Great by Ch. Chipiez

doing restoration works in Persepolis (see chapter 1.3) noticed that there had already been a former wall, not finished, in front of which the reliefs were set. Thus, the reliefs became a fundamental part of the building. The order in which the subject peoples are represented refers more or less to the order on the Tomb of Darius in Naqsh-e Rostam (no. 6.1). That suggests that the reliefs must have been made around the year 500 BC. The material of the administrative tablets from the archive of Darius found in a tower of the fortification walls of Persepolis reveals that in the year 499 BC thousands of additional workers were sent to Persepolis. And in that very year Farnaka, the marshal of the royal household, stayed most of the year in Persepolis while otherwise as a rule he always had to be next to the king. It seems that in this year the king wanted to push forward works in Persepolis. According to the plan of Darius only three buildings had to be on the Persepolis Terrace, the Apadana, the Palace and the Treasury (see fig. 6), as fourth we may assume an entrance-gate. Presumably, they were surrounded by gardens as evidenced by water-canals which are still to be traced on the Terrace. Already in Pasargadae it could be seen how important gardens were for the Achaemenids (see chapter 10). All the buildings on the Terrace of Persepolis served official requirements while the

8 / Reconstruction of the King receiving tributes by Madam Dieulafoy

palace where the king lived must have been somewhere on the plain. Remains of several palaces at the foot of the Terrace have been partly excavated but never published. Some parts of them are still to be seen in the south and north-west of the Terrace (see chapter 5).

The original plan of the Terrace was totally changed by Xerxes (486-465 BC). He not only finished the Apadana of his father (see no. 4.3), but he wanted to add extensive buildings of his own (fig. 9). For his large Palace with the so-called Harem buildings he found enough space only in the southern part of the Terrace between Darius-Palace (no. 4.5) and the Treasury (no. 4.13), where the way to the Apadana came up. So, he blocked the entrance from the south, filled in the gap in the wall with large stones and created a representative new stairway and gate in the north-west of the Terrace (no. 4.1). From this time on, every visitor has to enter the Terrace climbing up this staircase.

But, with this new entrance the situation on the Terrace changed. The gate through which a visitor passes leads nowhere. The main axis of the building, emphasized by the bulls on one and the man-bulls on the other side, is straight on. But, this does not make any sense because the buildings are to the right (fig. 9. 25 and 26). Only in a much later building-phase - especially after a dividing wall (A in fig. 9) had been built- a visitor was led in this direction towards the Hall of 100 Columns (no. 4.15) and the never finished gate (no. 4.17). This fact might suggest that Xerxes reused here at least the main parts of a gate made by Darius for his entrance from the south. There the direction of the building with a passing way leading straight onwards would have been perfectly fitting.

Xerxes added inscriptions of his own (XPa, see no. 4.1). When a visitor passed this gate he had to turn right and then he saw at first glance the northern side of the Apadana while the reliefs with the king and his peoples were around the corner of the building and not to be seen. And if this visitor had a look around this corner he would find the king turning his back towards him. This was an impossible situation. And so, Xerxes decided to copy the whole program of the eastern side in the mirror-view to the north. It can be traced in several instances that this was done in a haste. The proportions of figures on the reliefs are less well executed than on the eastern side. Finer incisions are missing in many cases (cf. fig. 12 and 13; 15 and 16) and some trees or rosettes on the bordering frames were not finished at all. these details were not that much obvious in former times because all the reliefs had been covered with bright colours. Now the northern side had to get a portico, too. To emphasize this

9 / Overall plan of the Terrace (after F. Krefter)

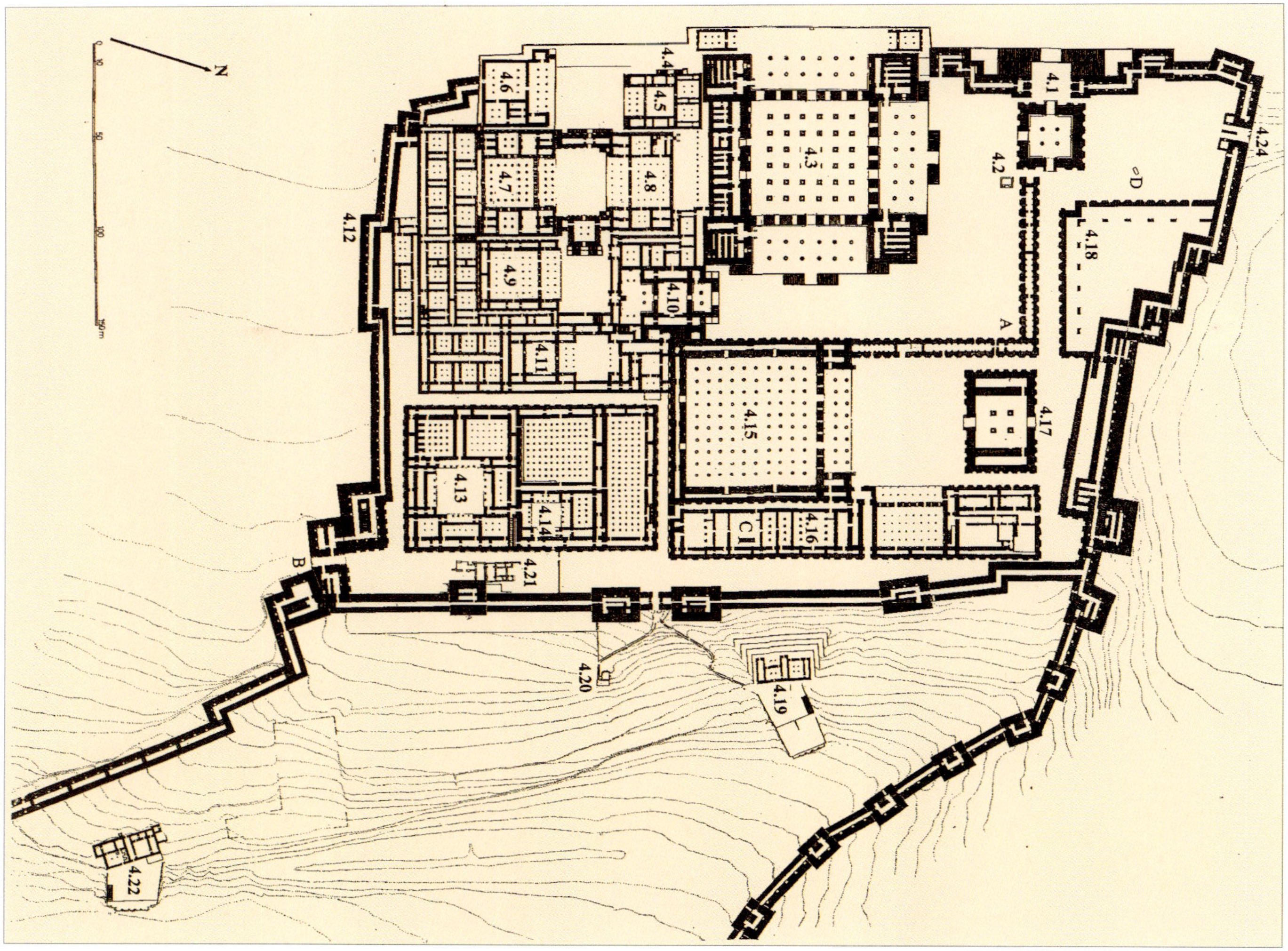

new entrance to the reception hall Xerxes chose columns of the same form as had been designed for the interior of the building, with the composite- and bull-capitals. In this way the newly created main facade of the Apadana looked rich and impressive, but there was no longer any difference between outer and inner columns and the well planned program of Darius lost its significance.

At first Xerxes had copied the central panel of the reliefs, too (the well preserved original is now in the Iran Bastan Museum in Tehran), but after a while he became annoyed by the sight of himself always standing behind the throne of his father. Wasn't he himself the king now for many years? And so he decided to remove the central reliefs on both sides and to replace them by neutral depictions of guardians, four on each side facing each other. But he did not dare to destroy the original centre-reliefs and so he put them on a less spectacular place, into the inner courtyard of the Treasury, where only few people were allowed to enter. There they were found during excavations and were called "Treasury- reliefs" before the Tilias found out their original position.

The reliefs of the so-called Hall of 100 Columns (no. 4.15) prove that it was indeed Xerxes who caused this replacement. This new reception-hall was built by Xerxes next to the Apadana; maybe it was his purpose to surpass his father. With its vast interior with 100 columns and many reliefs - all based on prototypes that had been created by Darius - it must have been an impressive building. In the northern and

10 / Reconstruction of the Treasury relief

11 / The Drangianians and Arachosians (delegation XV)

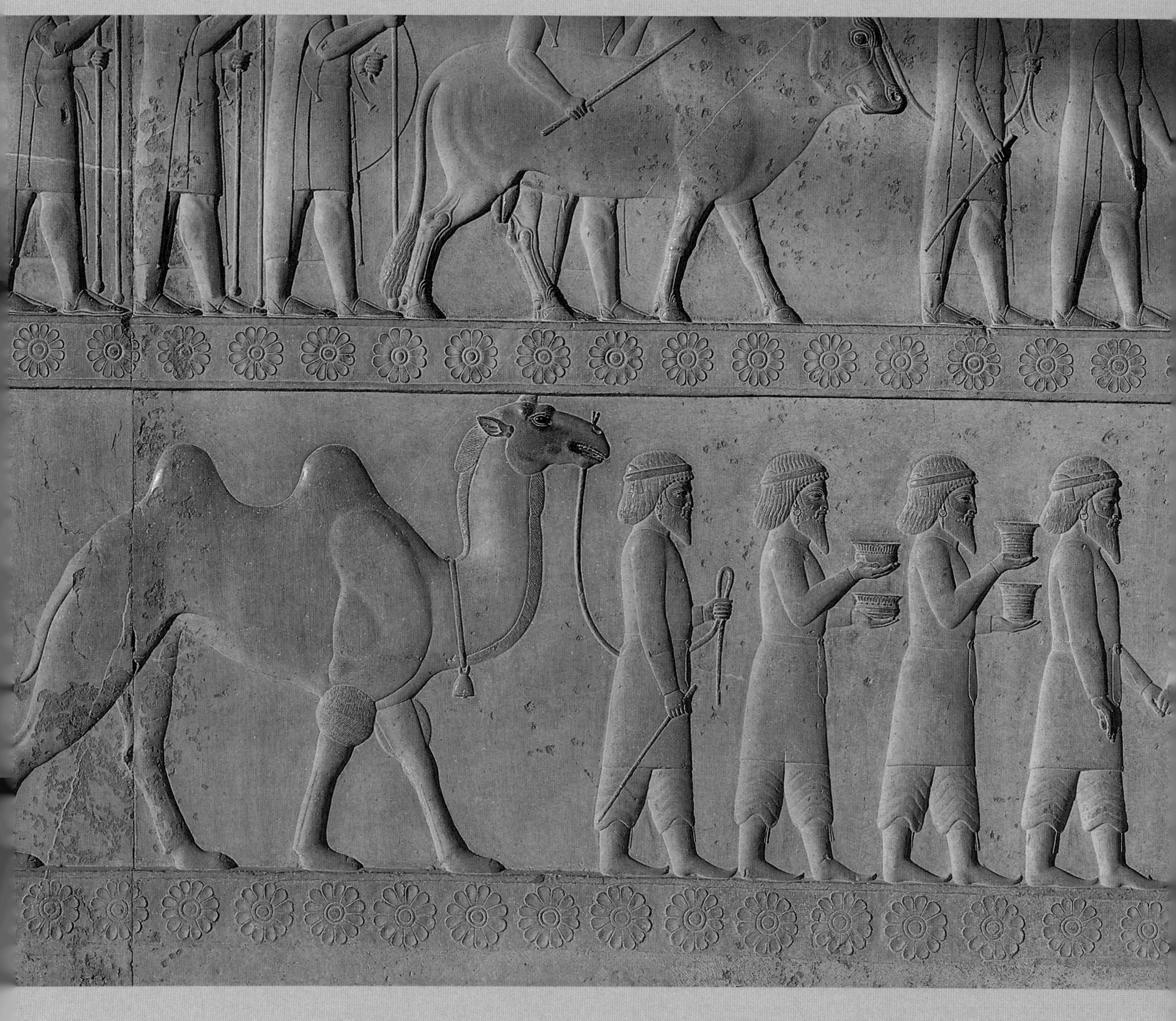

12 / Ionians with wool skeins from the northern Apadana staircase

13 / Scythians and Ionians with wool skeins (lower row)
from the eastern staircase

southern door-frames the king is depicted sitting on his throne - but without a crown-prince! He is replaced by a smaller figure of a servant with fly-whisk (fig. 147). Now Xerxes himself is sitting on the throne!

The Hall of 100 Columns was finished by Xerxes' son and successor Artaxerxes I (465-425/4 BC). He added then the so-called Tripylon (no. 4.10) between Apadana and Hall of 100 Columns to close the gap between these buildings and to create a passway between official and more private buildings. And he used reliefs with the former representation of king and crown-prince to decorate this building, because he did not feel any resentments against this motif.

During the reign of Artaxerxes the Terrace nearly got its final appearance. After that only few alterations and building activities took place. Artaxerxes III (359/8 –338/7BC) added the western staircase to the Palace of Darius and built another Palace in the south of the Apadana of which only little is left (no. 4.8). Though the Terrace was used during the whole Achaemenid reign and in parts also after the destruction by Alexander the Great in 331 BC, maybe well into Sassanian times, no later buildings can be identified. The date when the Gate of all Lands and the Hall of 100 Columns were connected with a mudbrick-wall (A in fig. 9), thus separating the north-eastern parts of the Terrace from the Apadana and connected buildings, is uncertain. Presumably, this must be seen in connection with the erection of another gate in front of the Hall of 100 Columns that was never finished (no. 4.17).

15 / The horses of the Lydians, detail of the eastern Apadana staircase

16 / The horses of the Lydians, detail of the northern Apadana staircase

4. Tour through the Ruins

For those visitors who have enough time it is advisable to start in the morning by climbing up to the first tomb to the north (see no. 4.19). From there one has a magnificent overview and can imagine the architectural development of different buildings on the Terrace.
Different monuments on the Terrace of Persepolis will be described according to a proposed tour. The visitor may choose an extensive tour with all the important monuments or a shorter one, indicated by an asterisk. The numbers correspond to those in the overall plan (see chapter 3).

*4.1. The Entrance to the Terrace: The Stairway and Gateway of All Lands (fig. 17 and 18)

The new road leads straight to the entrance which was built by Xerxes (486-465 BC). Still today every visitor enters the Terrace climbing the stairs to the Gateway of all Lands. The 7 m wide double-reversed stairway, made of huge stone-blocks, leads

14 / An overall view of the Terrace

first to the sides and then with a full turn back to the centre in front of the gate. There is a platform on its intermediate landings. It goes deeper in the width of the frontal stairs than the platform of the continuing stairs, thus creating a corner. This additional space with the corner may have been used for guardians, standing there to receive those who were arriving. Traces of parapets are to be seen at the outer edges of stairs and landings. The flights of steps show a gentle grade (fig. 17). It has been proposed that this would permit groups of horseman to ascend the Terrace. But, it is quite uncertain if this might have ever been allowed. The shallow steps may also have been considered more suitable for courtiers wearing the long court-costumes.

The entrance building is square (24,75 m). The doors and the four inner columns, that used to support the roof, are made of stone. The walls, made of sun-dried bricks with niches on the outside, are now missing. But, the door blocks were not smoothed to the right and left where the mud brick-wall was adjoined. The western door, facing the staircase, is adorned on both sides by huge bull sculptures (fig. 19) and the opposite eastern door by man-bulls wearing a horned feather-cap (fig. 20, 22 and 23).

17 / Looking from the Stairway : the Gateway of All Lands on the right.

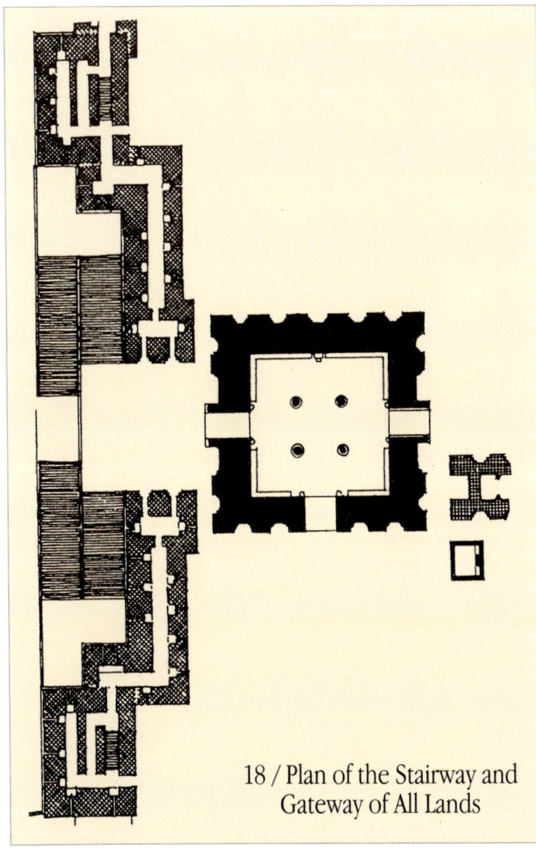
18 / Plan of the Stairway and Gateway of All Lands

The prototypes are clearly to be sought in Assyrian art and like there the front-part of the statues is given in full sculpture protruding from the walls while the larger part of the body with the hind legs is to be seen only in relief from the inner side of the doors. Above these reliefs are neatly chiselled inscriptions in Old Persian (XPa), always in the middle, Elamite and Babylonian at the outer sides.

"The Great God is Ahura Mazda, who created this earth, who created yonder sky, who created man, who created happiness for man, who made Xerxes king, the one king of many, the one master of many. I am Xerxes, the Great King, King of Kings, King of lands containing all kinds of men, King on this great earth even far off, King Darius' son, an Achaemenid.
Proclaims Xerxes, the King: By the will of Ahura Mazda, this Gateway of All Lands I built. Much other beautiful was made within this Persepolis, which I made and which my father made. Whatever appears (to be) beautiful, all that we built by the will of Ahura Mazda.
Proclaims Xerxes, the King: Me may Ahura Mazda protect, and my kingdom, and what was made by me, and what was made by my father, that also may Ahura Mazda protect!"
So, Xerxes himself gave the gate its name. The two sculptured doors emphasize a pass-way that leads straight onwards and not into the direction of the main-building - the Apadana. This might suggest, that the gate originally belonged to Darius' entrance in the south of the Terrace and was removed by Xerxes (for further discussion of this problem, see chapter 3). A third door of which nearly nothing is preserved led directly to the northern side of the Apadana (fig. 25). It is wider (5,15 m) than the other two doors (3,8 m). But on the inner side of the door-frame there are remains of stone-slabs encircled by a rosette ornament around the pivots. So, there

must have been a huge door of two leaves, nearly 12 m high, presumably made of wood and adorned with gilded bronze sheets. This door, so very different from the other two, might have been added to the original plan, since it was needed to direct the visitor towards the new facade of the Apadana created by Xerxes. Comparable ornamented stone-slabs were found at the inner side of the eastern doorway, too, so that we can assume that the whole building could be locked. The architrave of the eastern doorway could be restored from pieces lying on the ground. Its total length is 8,08 m, its height 1,75 m and it weighs nearly 25 tons. The architraves were crowned - to the internal as well as to external sides - by cornice elements, a piece of which has been restored on the top of the eastern architrave. There are stone-benches along the inner walls of the gate, maybe for waiting visitors. The seat exactly opposite the southern door is emphasised by a step to rest one's feet. Slim columns, 16,5 m high, are similar to the columns of the hall of the Apadana. The bases are covered with sharply cut leaves. The composite-capitals look like chalices of lotus flowers on which a square part, richly decorated with flutes and volutes, supports the final capitals with addorsed bulls (fig. 21). Their heads were looking towards the south and north, thus a visitor, entering from the large stairway could see them in full size.

19 / The western door of the Gateway of All Lands

4.2. The Water Basin

At the south-eastern corner of the Gateway of all Lands (fig. 18) there is a huge water basin (4 by 4 m) made of stone. It is 1,2 m deep inside its western part, and the eastern part is only 46 cm with two narrow ramps ascending to a small platform. Water canals are leading from there over the Terrace.

*4.3. The Apadana (fig. 24 and 27)

Due to the alterations by Xerxes the northern side of the Apadana became the main facade (see chapter 3). But, the originals of the reliefs are to be seen on the eastern side of the building, where one can imagine the idea of the whole program. The reliefs there are much more finely executed and better preserved. Therefore, it is advisable to proceed to the eastern side which is nowadays protected by a metal-roof which, unfortunately, spoils much of the former impression of the building. The palaces of Cyrus the Great (555-530 BC, see nos. 10.3 and 10.4) in Pasargadae must have been the prototype for this reception hall. But, this building in Persepolis is definitely an improvement. While the porticoes of the palaces in Pasargadae reach only one third of the height of the building, here they are as high as the whole building. Thus, there are 12 about 20 m high stone-columns in two rows on the western side as well as on the eastern side. The western side of the building lay directly above the 15 m high supporting walls of the Terrace (fig. 77.). So, the columns seemed to scratch the sky and they could be seen already far away across the plain. This is the conception of later Greek temples as on the Acropolis of Athens or in Asia Minor. But here, in Persepolis, we find it for the first time. And it must have been an idea of Darius and his consulting architects.

While the western portico was meant to impress those who were outside the Terrace, the eastern portico was the main facade on the Terrace (fig. 28). This can be seen in several respects. All corners of the building were secured by protruding towers. They were made - as all the walls - of mud bricks and adorned with glazed bricks, remains of which are to be seen in the corridors of the eastern outer side of the museum. The bricks showed not only ornaments with lotus flowers (fig. 32) but also an inscription of which only fragments are preserved (XPg): *"Proclaims Xerxes, the Great King: By the will of Ahura Mazda much that (is) good did Darius, the King, who (was) my father, build and plan. Also by the will of Ahura Mazda I added to that work and built more. Me may Ahura Mazda protect, together with the gods, and my kingdom!"*

20 / The eastern door of the Gateway of All Lands

21 / A view of the Gateway of All Lands

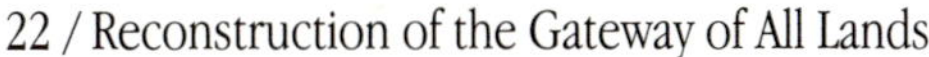

22 / Reconstruction of the Gateway of All Lands

23 / Drawing of the eastern door of the Gateway of All Lands

The foundation inscriptions of Darius the Great were found in the two towers to the right and the left side of the eastern facade. This situation emphasizes the importance of this side, too. On both sides a silver and a golden tablet were put into a stone-box. These four plaques were 33 by 33 cm, which means the same size as all the bricks which were used for the building. The inscriptions are identical, again in Old Persian, Elamite and Babylonian:

"*Darius, the Great King, King of Kings, King of lands, the son of Hystaspes, an Achaemenid. Proclaims Darius, the King: This kingdom which I hold, from the Scythians who are beyond Sogdiana, from there as far as Ethiopia, from India, from there as far as Lydia, Ahura Mazda the greatest of the gods bestowed upon me. Me may Ahura Mazda protect and my royal house!*" The Apadana building is erected on a high platform which consists of a core of bedrock, thus raising it from its surroundings. Four symmetrically arranged flights of 31 steps lead up to the portico, dividing the whole facade into three equal portions (fig. 27).

24 / A view of the columns of the Apadana

25 / View from the southern door of the Gateway of All Lands towards the Apadana

The central flights - which occupy one third - are the most prominent. The facades and parapets of the stairways are covered with reliefs. The central relief with an empty panel in the middle shows now four soldiers, facing one another on each side of the panel. They are alternately clothed in the Achaemenid court-costume with long folds and long sleeves and a feather-cap and the Iranian riding-costume with trousers and a rounded fell-cap with an animal's tail as pendant. The shields show a characteristic form with oval apertures on both long-sides and a buckle in the middle. They must have been composed of wood and leather with metal buckle. This relief had been put in by Xerxes when he brought the original one to the Treasury where it is still to be seen (fig. 10 and 129 ff.) (see chapter 3 and the description no. 4. 14). Originally, here was the focus of the whole program: the king amidst all his subjects who were arriving from one side (left) and the guards and dignitaries on the other side (right). Above the scene is a winged sun-symbol, flanked by male sphinxes with leonine bodies. The spaces below the wings and in the back of the sphinxes are filled with lotus flowers. These reliefs were inserted together with the new central panel. Two blocks of the former baldachin, under which the king was sitting, have been found reused at the stairway of Palace G (no. 4.8). The central relief is flanked on both sides by a symbolical representation of a lion defeating a bull (fig. 36). The meaning of this symbol which occurs very often on the reliefs of the Terrace is not yet certain. But it has been known in Iran since the 4th millennium BC and seems to represent the powers of day and night fighting again and again with each other. To the sides are ornaments of lotus flowers, which become smaller and smaller towards the bottom of the stairs.

On the left wing of the staircase various peoples of the Achaemenid empire coming towards their king and bringing him their best gifts are depicted. They arrive from the southern side where the entrance to the Terrace was in Darius' time (see chapter 3), thus taking the same way as every visitor did. On the other hand when seeing the reliefs the visitor got the feeling that he was joining a stream of people all longing to meet their king who was waiting for them in the centre.The subject peoples are depicted in three registers, at the beginning and in the end following the descending staircase. Different peoples are divided by trees in blossom. Each delegation is introduced by a Persian usher alternately clad either in the Persian court-dress and a high cap, sometimes adorned with feathers, or the Iranian riding-costume with trousers and felt-cap.

To the latter outfit belonged the Iranian short sword, the *akinakes*, which was fixed with a hanging on the belt and fastened around the right thigh, while the court-dress was always combined with the dagger stuck in front behind the belt. In older literature these two forms of garment were considered to identify the Persians - those with the long folded dress - and the Medes - with the riding costume.

26 / Overall view of the northern Apadana staircase

And the appearance of both, alternating with each other, has been explained as Darius' wish to show that the Medes are equally valued as the Persians in his empire. But this view cannot hold any longer. It is more likely that all those people are Persians just wearing two different types of garment. It is obvious that all those who were working in some way like the horse-grooms (right side of the upper register on the right side of the stairs) and all the attendants are wearing the riding-costume. Not all the peoples on the reliefs can be identified with certainty because there are no inscriptions. A great help are the representations of all nations on the tomb of Darius which are inscribed.

Peoples are mostly discerned by their characteristic features and clothes, but some of them are so similar to one another or without any obvious details that there are still many discussions about the identity of some of them. The scheme (fig. 37) gives the most appropriate identification for the time being. The map (fig. 41) shows the provinces of the empire where the peoples are coming from.

The most important peoples of the empire, the Medes and the Elamites, are at the beginning in the upper row, the Babylonians are in the middle. But because of the decline of the stairs there was still a small space in front of them, where the Armenians were put in, though they belong to the peoples of the lower row, in which the Lydians are leading, as the most important and the richest people of the west. When we now have a closer look at the reliefs, admire the fine workmanship and the rendering of all the tiny details we should always keep in mind, that originally the reliefs were painted in bright colours, dazzling the view with additional painted motifs and surely highlighted with gold on all the precious vessels, bracelets and so on.

I. The Medes (fig. 44)
They are introduced by a Persian usher in court-dress. He grasps the hand of the delegation-leader. All the delegations are headed by such a leader, who sometimes is armed or clad a bit differently from the following members of the delegation and who never carries any gift. The Medes are clad in Iranian riding-costumes with trousers. The last three of the delegation bring a whole set of such a costume as gift. We can clearly discern the different pieces belonging to it: an upper garment hanging down to the knees, with long sleeves; an overcoat, the so-called *kandys*, of which the sleeves are so narrow that it is impossible to slip into them; and panty hoses as here can be clearly seen (cf. fig. 43). This garment is worn by several peoples (confer delegations III, IV, IX, XI, XVI) while some others are dressed in similar one. But, they all are discerned by their headgear though it is of the same type, generally

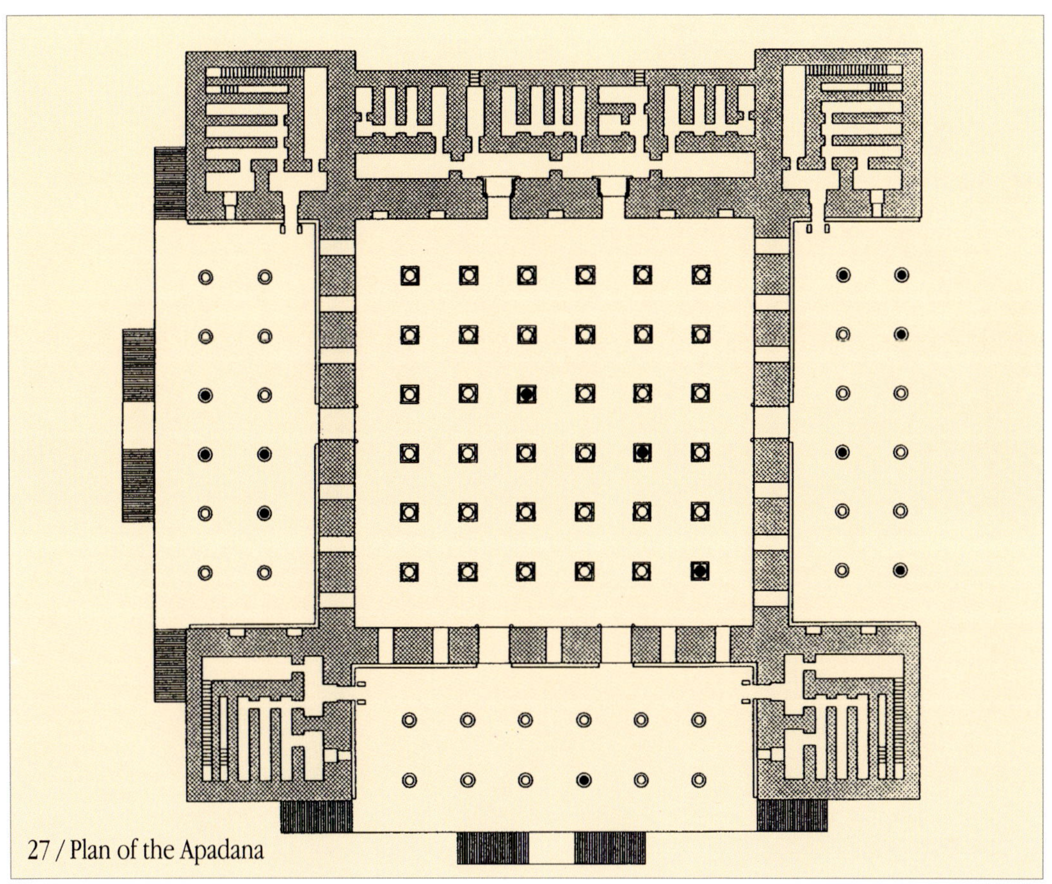
27 / Plan of the Apadana

called with the Turkish word *bashlyk*. This might have been the same headgear that appears in Greek sources as tiara. It hangs down the neck and could be closed over the mouth. The headgear of the Medes is topped by three knobs and has a long tip that covers the hair which is falling down on the shoulders. Only the first member of the delegation wears the round cap which is usually combined with the riding-costume. Other gifts of the Medes are a pitcher, two beakers, a short sword (*akinakes*) and two pairs of bracelets. In one case the endings of the latter are only given in contour-lines, while the surface is roughened. Presumably, there had been fixed animal-heads in another material. The forms of all the objects, which must have been of precious metal, are typically Achaemenid. In his building inscription from Susa Darius refers to the Medes as goldsmiths (see chapter 3).

28 / The eastern side of the Apadana

II. The Elamites (fig. 42 and 51)

The Elamites wear a long folded dress. This was originally a typical Elamite dress which was taken over by the Persians who made it their court-gown. The third member of the Elamite delegation carries two of those daggers which were always combined with this kind of dress. Around their short curly hair the Elamites wear a fillet which is tied with a loop or a loose end in the back of their head. The shoes of the Elamites with their tiny buttons holding the straps are very similar to the Persian shoes, but those of the Elamites are always little boots reaching up to the ankles with six straps while those of the Persians have only three. Besides the sheathed daggers the Elamites present bows ending in ducks' heads. They were popular among the Persians too, as can be seen on the reliefs of the dignitaries. The lioness, looking back at her two cubs, was destined for the king's hunting ground, which the Persians called paradeisos. This meant an enclosed area and is the origin of our word "paradise".

29 / Fanciful drawing of the Apadana by Ch. Chipiez

30 / Fanciful drawing of the Apadana by Ch. Chipiez

IV. The Parthians (fig. 45)

They lived on the southern shores of the Caspian Sea and wore the Iranian riding-costume too, but combined with boots. Their leader put the *kandys* around his shoulders. Their heads are totally wrapped by the *bashlyks*, one end hanging down their back. They offer precious beakers, a Bactrian two-humped camel and a feline skin.

31 / Fanciful reconstruction of the Apadana and the Hall of Xerxes by Ch. Chipiez

32 / Brick decoration from the Apadana

VII. The Aryans

The Aryans from the east, in the region around the city of Herat, wear special *bashlyks*, which are folded in three layers around their heads and end at the top nearly horizontally with a small conical projection. The trousers are notched at the sides and strapped under the knees. They bulge over the high boots with slightly upturned tips. The gifts are similar to those of the Parthians, but the beakers have another shape.

33 / Reliefs of Persian soldiers on the inner side of the Apadana stairway walls

34 / Glazed-brick friezes from the Darius Palace at Susa

35 / Reliefs of the Lotus flowers

36 / Lion defeating a bull, relief from the eastern Apadana stairway

37 / Scheme of the peoples represented on the eastern Apadana stairway

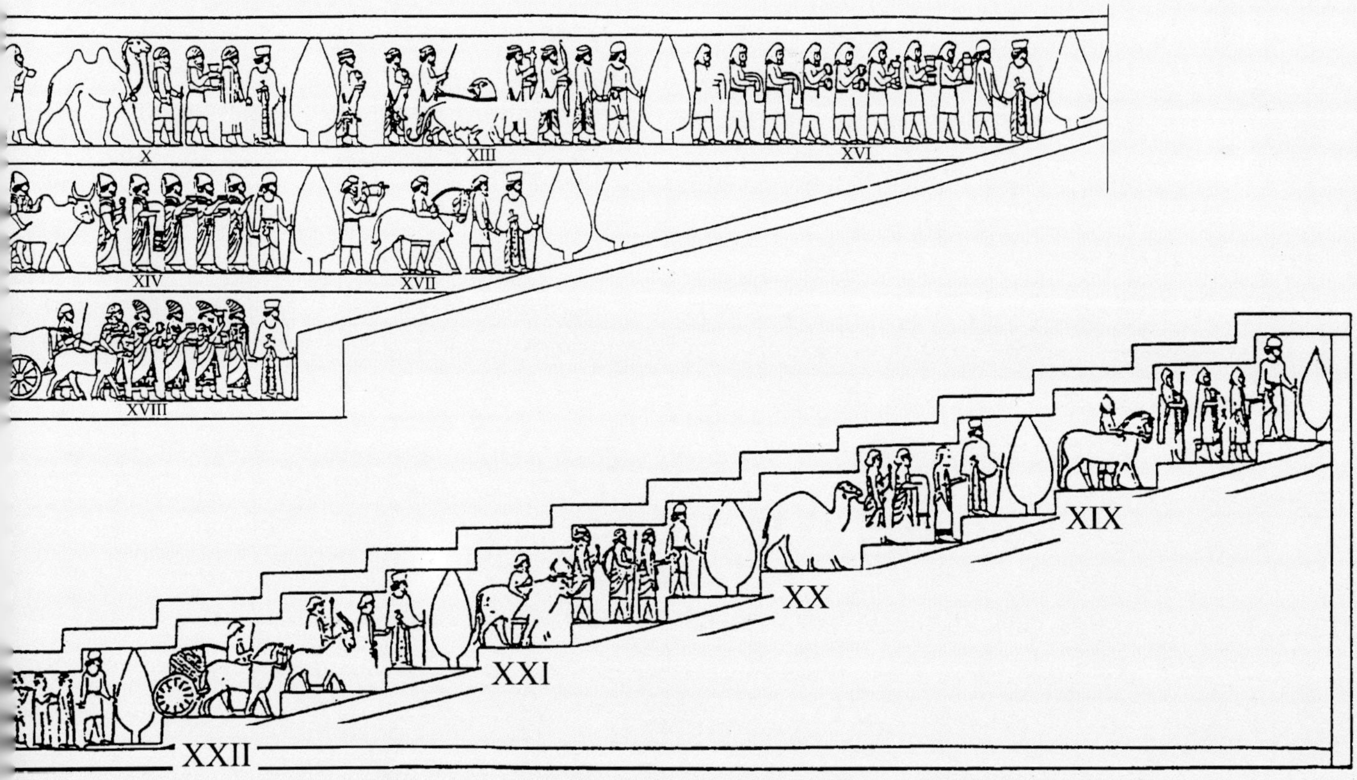

X XIII XVI

XIV XVII

XVIII

XIX

XX

XXI

XXII

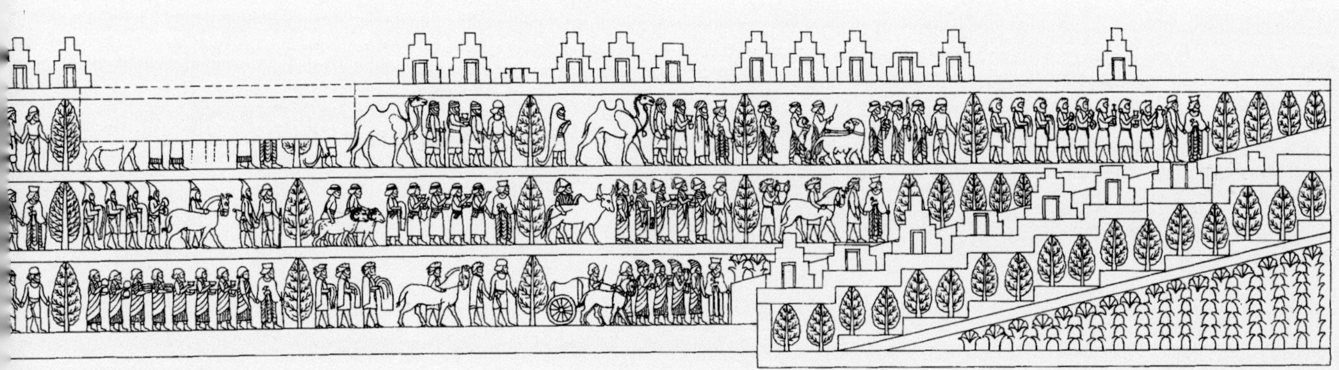

38 / Glazed-brick friezes from the Darius Palace at Susa, Iran Bastan Museum, Tehran

39 / Glazed-brick friezes from the Darius Palace at Susa, Iran Bastan Museum, Tehran

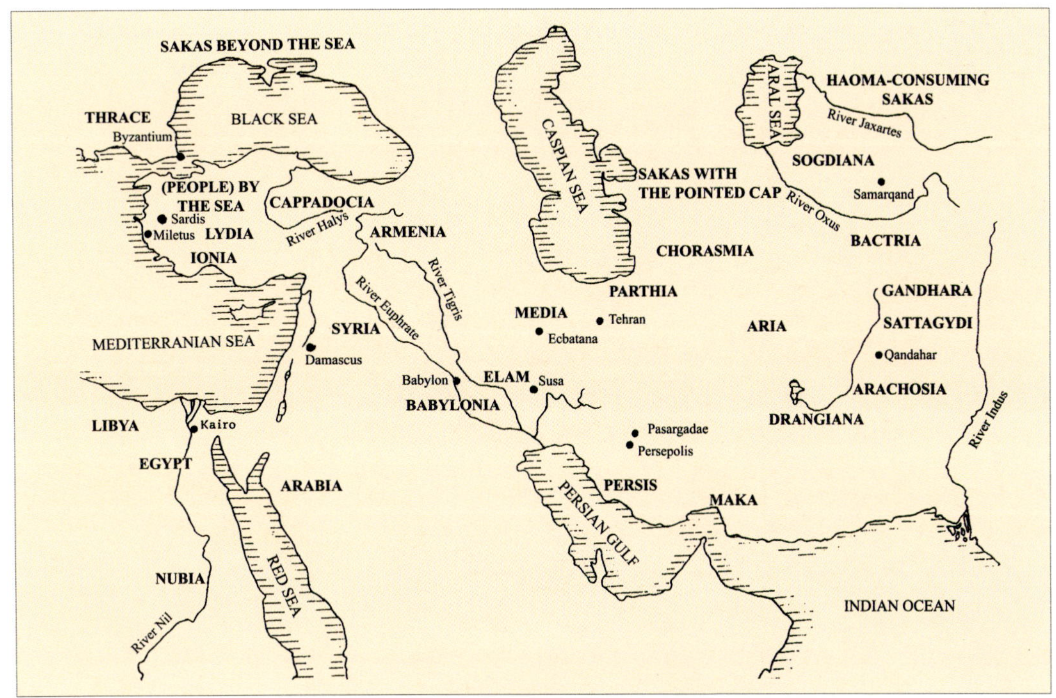

41 / The provinces of the Achaemenid Empire

X. The Egyptians

The following field is badly destroyed, just the feet are preserved. The people are barefoot, their long gowns ending with fringes. A similar garment is worn by the Egyptian representative on the tomb of Darius, so this delegation can be identified. Of all their gifts only the end of a folded fabric and the feet of a huge bull are discernible.

XIII. The Bactrians

Like their neighbours, the Parthians and Aryans, they bring a Bactrian camel and precious bowls. Their garments are comparable to that of the Medes but the trousers are baggy. They don't wear a headgear. Their curl-bunches are covered and bound up with a fine cloth. This feature is typical of the Bactrians and helps to identify this delegation.

40 / General view of the Terrace

42 / The Elamites (delegation II) (upper row), and the Armenians (delegation III) (lower row)

43 / Bracelets and a set of the Iranian riding costume brought by the Scythians (upper row), and the Ionians (delegation XII) (lower row)

XVI. The Sagartians (fig. 46)

Another people in Iranian riding-costume follow at the end of the upper register. Some of them are dressed like the Medes, others like the Armenians. They again present a whole set of riding-costume and a horse with its hair bound in a bunch between the ears and with the end of the tail bound up. This is characteristic of Achaemenid horses. These people might represent the Sagartians who lived in the western part of Media and were famous for their special troops handling the lasso.

44 / The Medes (delegation I)

III. The Armenians (fig. 42)

The middle row starts with a small field with the Armenians. They are dressed like the Medes but have raised their cheek-flaps and tied them at the back of their heads. They offer a horse and a beautiful amphora with griffin-handles. The spout leads through the body of the animal to the right. This is a typical Achaemenid form of a vessel.

In this case the corresponding relief of the northern stairway is different. There is no horse, but instead four tribute-bearers. Three of them are offering a set of the Iranian riding-costume, the fourth two beakers (the upper one on a stone patch set into the surface) - a rather insignificant representation.

V. The Babylonians (fig. 47)

The first large field of the middle register is occupied by the Babylonians. Their heads are covered with conical caps with a long tip suspended behind. Their overcoats consist of a long scarf which is wrapped around their bodies, the tasselled end thrown forward over the right shoulder. The first two gift-bearers carry a bowl in each hand, the third one brings a long scarf, ending in network with tassels. In addition the Babylonians present a humped bull.

VIII. The Syrians (fig. 49)

The Syrians wear a plain dress with a sash around their waists and low boots with tongue and four straps with a double loop at the front of the bootleg. They also bring precious bowls. The third gift-bearer carries animal-skins which look rather plain and stiff. These may have been bronze-ingots in the shape of animal-skins,

45 / The Parthians (delegation IV)

because the Syrian bronze-mines of the Hauran were famous. The next gift seems to be a Syrian dress at the corners of which are tiny lead-weights to insure its falling down in the right way. Two beautiful rams are at the end.

46 / The Sagartians (delegation XVI)

XI. The Scythians (fig. 43)

The next delegation wears peculiar high pointed bashlyks. Therefore, they were called "Sakas (= Scythians) with the pointed cap" by the Persians. In this case they represent the other Scythian peoples too, so for instance, those who were called "hauma-consuming Sakas". Hauma was an intoxicating drink of Iranian people which, presumably, was extracted from mushrooms (fly-fungus) and played an important role in religion, too. The Scythians are all armed, wearing their characteristic short swords, the *akinakes*, and the leader the typical bow-case, the *gorytos*, ending in a bird's head. The Scythians present a fine bridled horse with a bell around its neck, a pair of bracelets and again a full set of Iranian riding-costume.

XIV. The Sattagydians and Gandarians (fig. 56)

The two peoples are here presumably combined in one field, because they used to wear the same clothes with short-sleeved coat and broad belt. Their legs are bare, but they wear sandals with heel guards. They offer a humped bull, spears and a round shield.

XVII. The Sogdians and Chorasmians (fig. 52)

Once again two peoples who are very close to each other are put together in the last field of the middle register. The shape of their *bashlyks* with a rounded anterior

47 / The Babylonians (delegation V)

point is typical for them. The overcoat is slanting to the back. The strap guard in front of the belts is composed of two joined deer legs (like that one of the royal bow-case on the "Treasury-relief", see no. 4.14). They present a short sword (***akinakes***) like the one which they themselves as well as the Scythian delegation are wearing and which is offered by the Medes. The other gifts are a pair of bracelets, battle-axes and again a horse.

VI. The Lydians (fig. 55)

The lower row starts at the right with the most important people from the west. They wear peculiar conical twisted caps and a little braid of hair behind the ear which helps to recognize them as Lydians. The short-sleeved garments show a wavy pattern, which might indicate wool. A scarf is wrapped around the body and thrown over the left shoulder. The tips of the low boots are slightly turned upwards. The precious amphorae are similar to the Armenian amphora - except for the flutes in the lower part. They bring bowls, too, and a pair of extraordinary bracelets ending in griffins. These bracelets are very flat and seem to represent a special Lydian kind which was inlaid with glass (fig. 57). A pair of stallions with fine harnesses draws a chariot (compare the exquisite execution of the horse-heads with those of the northern stairway) . The axle-pin decorated with a tiny figure shows how beautiful the whole chariot must have been (compare the chariots of the king on the right end of the east-side, see description below). The very gifts reveal how rich these people were.

IX. The Cappadocians (fig. 60)

The Cappadocians are clad like the Armenians who were their neighbours. But, in addition they wear capes which are fastened under their right shoulders with a Phrygian fibula. They bring a horse, too, and another Iranian riding-costume.

XII. The Ionians (fig. 43)

The clothes of the Ionians resemble those of the Lydians. They may have been made of wool, and wool skeins and fine folded clothes belong also to the gifts which are presented here. They carry precious beakers and bowls. Figs. 12 and 13 again show the differences in the execution of eastern and northern staircase of the Apadana. Look for instance at the heads and wool skeins!

XV. The Drangianians and Arachosians (fig. 56)

These two peoples wearing the same type of clothes are again represented together. Their trousers are extremely baggy falling down in heavy waves. The beakers and bowls are of the finest workmanship (fig. 61) - as their earrings are. And they bring another Bactrian camel.

48 / Armenian (delegation III), detail of fig. 42

49 / The Syrians (delegation VIII) presenting rams

XVIII. The Indians (fig. 52)

Coming from warm regions of the Indus River they are barefoot and wear just dhotis except for their leader who wears sandals and has wrapped a cloth around his body to appear more properly dressed in the presence of the king. The first gift-bearer carries a stick above his shoulders with suspending baskets. There are two pouches in each basket which may contain the famous gold-dust of the Indus-valley. The others bring a donkey and double-edged battle-axes.

The main-field of the reliefs of the subject peoples is bordered to the left by an inscription-panel which had been inscribed by Xerxes (XPb). The Old Persian version is here and again on the right panel of the northern stairway, while the Elamite and Babylonian versions are together on the corresponding panel in the northern part of the eastern stairway. They are missing on the northern façade (see 4.1). The beginning of the inscription is the same as on the Gateway of All Lands, then it continues: "*Proclaims Xerxes, the Great King: That what has been built by me here and what has been built by me more distant, all that by the will of Ahura Mazda I made. Me*

50 / Reliefs of Persian soldiers on the inner side of the Apadana stairway walls

may Ahura Mazda protect together with the gods, and my kingdom, and my work!" It is striking that in this inscription Xerxes did not mention his father as builder (which he does on the tiles which adorned the towers, see below). But on the other hand he was not lying and claiming that the entire building was done by himself. He had chosen a very diplomatic formulation. This might be a hint, that the inscriptions were added after he had removed the main-panels of the stairways, that is, in the time when he did not want to emphasize too much the deeds of his father. Again a group of lion and bull follows and - where the stairs decline - remaining peoples are depicted:

XIX. The Thracians (fig. 53)
They wear slightly pointed bashlyks with ear-flaps and bring their characteristic wicker-shields and a pair of lances together with a bridled horse.

XX. The Arabians (fig. 54)
They have only light clothes wrapped around their bodies and wear sandals. The lower border of the leader's garment is embroidered. Presumably, they offer to the king a fine example of their clothes as well as a dromedary.

XXI. The Carians (fig. 65)
The next people might be the Carians because their cloaks are comparable to those of the Lydians and Ionians though they are wearing trousers. They offer a circular shield with spear and a bull with finely curved horns.

XXII. The Libyans (fig. 66)
Characteristic are their fringed garments which look as if they were made from felt. They bring a lance, a goat (antelope?) with beautiful horns and a pair of horses drawing a chariot.

XXIII. The Ethiopians (fig. 67)
The last ones are the Ethiopians. Because of the landing of the staircase their figures are rather small. They are clearly discernible by their curled hair and Negroid features. They bring a covered bowl, an elephant tusk and an okapi.
These are the peoples of the vast Persian Empire who are coming to see their king, to pay him homage and to bring their best gifts. In contrast to Assyrian palace reliefs, here no battles or captives are rendered, and the main impression is, that all the peoples come by their own free will and they may also wear their weapons in the presence of the king.

51 / The Elamites presenting a lioness with her cubs

The reliefs on the right, in the back of the king, are the counterparts to these illustrations. And here are indeed represented those who are backing up the power of the king. Again there are three registers. Nearly a half of all the three is covered by the guards of the king. These are the famous "apple-bearers" because their lances end in a golden or silver pomegranate (fig. 68.). In order to protect this precious little apple they put it on their forward foot and not directly on the earth. One has often assumed that these guards were Elamites because they are dressed like the Elamite delegation and wear a fillet around their heads. But, this fillet is twisted and no knot is visible. And most important, these guards wear the Persian shoes with only three straps. So, we can be sure that all these soldiers were Persians; the king would not have put his safety into the hands of Elamites! In this case the guardians are not in a battle but surround the king on the occasion of a peaceful event, therefore, they are wearing the court-dresses.All those who had to provide facilities if the king wanted to move either on horseback or in a chariot are depicted in the second part of the upper row. They are all dressed in the riding-costumes. The first man bears a staff which may have been a badge, showing that he was subordinate to the marshal of the royal household. He is followed by four men with a carpet or a saddle-cloth folded under their arms and whips in their hands. The last one is carrying the king's chariot-stool in addition. The second man with a staff, presumably the court-equerry, is standing in front of three servants, each leading a horse. Still in Safavid times it was customary to bring always three horses before the king so that he might have the choice. The third group is also headed by a man with the staff, this time clad in the court-dress. He is followed by two pairs of horses with chariots and charioteers. The first chariot is more richly adorned, showing a lozenge pattern framed by rows of walking lions, and must, therefore, have been the king's one. The second one may have been for the crown-prince. The object hanging to the side of both chariots is probably a bow-case. The wheels are studded with nails and show 12 spindle-shaped spokes. The axle pin is decorated with a small human figure.

52/The Sogdians (delegation XVII) (upper row), and the Indians (delegation XVIII) (lower row)

53 / The Thracians (delegation XIX)

54 / The Arabians (delegation XX)

The two lower registers are filled with Persian dignitaries and functionaries who are alternately clad into the court-dresses and the riding-costumes with fitting armours (fig. 71). They are richly adorned with plain or twisted torques, earrings and bracelets. Some hold a flower in their hands, in some cases a globular bud. Here and there, one of them looks backward and seems to be speaking with his neighbour, or they put their arms on shoulders of companions. These postures bring some life into the picture. But, on the other hand these rows seem to be rendered on purpose, for the soldiers, the dignitaries and the functionaries are the pillars of the realm, like columns they are supporting the building of the empire. All those represented on the staircase reliefs - the subject peoples on one side, those who are responsible for functioning of law and order on the other side and the king in the middle - are the foundations of the Achaemenid empire which is symbolized by the building of the Apadana. Thus, it is really a "state-building".

55 / The Lydians (delegation VI)

The reliefs of the north-side of the Apadana were copied in the mirror-view by Xerxes when he built his new entrance (see chapter 3). They can be identified according to the description of the eastern side though there are minor variations. But they are less carefully executed and less well preserved (cf. fig. 12, 15, 16). Standing in front of the eastern side we can see to the left the so-called Tripylon which will be described later-on (see no. 4.10). We continue the way through the ruins by climbing up the stairs to get on the floor level of the building. In doing so we are accompanied on both sides by guards on parapet reliefs, crowned by four-stepped crenelations. (fig. 33 and 50) Then, we find ourselves standing in the eastern portico which stretches between the corner towers. Once the roof was supported by 12 columns in two rows. These columns are the most beautiful in the whole building (fig. 63, 64). The bell-shaped bases are covered with lotus flowers hanging downwards; between them palmettos are raised. Nearly 20 m high columns are very slim and composed of large drums, up to 8 m high, which become smaller towards the top. The columns of the Apadana

56 / The Sattagydians and Gandarians (delegation XIV) (upper row),
The Drangianians and Arachosians bringing a Bactrian camel (delegation XV) (lower row)

58 / Golden bracelet

57 / The Lydians (delegation VI) presenting bracelets

60 / The Cappadocians (delegation IX)

59 / Glass bracelet

63 / Detail of the capital in the form of addorsed lion-griffins from the eastern Apadana portico

61 / Detail of the Drangianians and Arachosians bringing goblets

62 / Detail of the Drangianians and Arachosians bringing bowls

64 / Capitals in the form of addorsed lion-griffins from the eastern Apadana portico

65 / The Carians (delegation XXI)

66 / The Libyans (delegation XXII)

67 / The Ethiopians bringing an elephant tusk and an okapi

68 / The "apple-bearers", guards of the king, from the eastern Apadana staircase

69 / A Persian dignitary

70 / Persian guards on the southern face of the northern Apadana stairways

71 / Detail of Persian dignitaries from the right lower register of the eastern Apadana stairway

show the most numerous flutes, 48 and one column in the eastern portico even 52, while the other buildings show only 40 (Gateway of all Lands, no. 4.1) or 36 (Hall of 100 Columns, no. 4.15). The capitals were in the form ofaddorsed lion-griffins (fig. 63 and 64), two of them looking into opposite direction, which means, originally to the south and the north of the building. They also appear only in the eastern portico. Their impressive parts are still to be seen. The horns had been fixed separately as can be seen at the cleanly cut square holes which were prepared for fastening them. Large beams of the ceiling rested on one side on the walls of the hall and led then across the back of the animals. A second beam, a bit thicker than the first one, was always put above. This construction is quite clearly discernible on the tomb-facades (fig. 155.) .The heads of the beams must have been ornamented, coloured or covered with metal-sheets. The distance between the columns was 8,65 m, that means that the beams must have been more than 20 m long. Presumably, Darius had ordered cedars from Lebanon for these beams, as he reported in his Susa-inscription (see chapter 3). And indeed, burned cedar-wood has been found during the excavations in Persepolis. On these heavy girders smaller ones were laid, resting on the heads of the lion-griffins. The ceiling as well as the lion-griffins and the column-bases must have been painted in bright colours, too. The lion-griffins and the addorsed bulls of the other capitals (one well preserved example in the courtyard of the Museum), (see no. 4.11) had red eyes, tongues and nostrils, the curls were painted blue and were supposed to imitate lapis lazuli, which was used in reality on precious statues, for hair and beards. Fragments of lapis lazuli-beards were found in Persepolis, too. The hoofs were presumably gilded.

The walls of the Apadana-hall had been made of sun-dried bricks which are now missing. Their former place and extension is today indicated by low brick-walls. They were 5,32 m thick, covered with plaster. The corner-towers were adorned with glazed bricks (fig. 32, see outside of Museums building, no. 4.11). Some of them were part of an inscription which has been reconstructed. In it Xerxes states: "*By the will of Ahura Mazda, King Darius my father built and ordered much good. By the will of Ahura Mazda I added to that construction and built further.*"

The inner walls of the porticoes and inside the building may have been covered with wall paintings which already had a long tradition in Assyrian art. Unfortunately, nothing is preserved in the Apadana, because all was destroyed by a violent conflagration. It must have been that one which the soldiers of Alexander the Great

72 / Persian soldiers reconstructed by Madame Dieulafoy

kindled in 331 BC. But, small fragments of wall painting have been found in Pasargadae (cf. also the Treasury, no. 4.13). From comparison with the other buildings in Persepolis it can be assumed that windows were set into the walls. In the southern portion of the eastern portico, remains of a mud-brick bench were discovered, which was set against the walls and, presumably, continued along the walls of the entire portico. The entrance to the Apadana-hall on the eastern side is 5,25 m wide, nearly as much as the walls are thick. That means that the passageway between the portico and the hall was 28 m^2. This space was covered by thick, square flags, made of dark stone (fig. 73) and put into a bitumen-layer. They were ornamented with flat rosettes and circles so that the whole looked like a carpet. On the inner side the entrance could be closed by a two-leafed door. The holes for the pivots with fine decorations (restored) are still to be seen. Their diameter was 21,5 cm and the hinges must have been of metal to hold the heavy doors. We can imagine that the door was of wood but richly ornamented with gilded bronze-sheets. Two pieces of a bronze-band with rosettes have been found in the Apadana, but it is not sure whether they belonged to the door.

The hall was square, each side 60,50 m. The roof was supported by 6 by 6 rows of columns (fig. 78). Their bases were not ornamented as in the porticoes but were square, two stepped plinths carrying a discoid torus. The column-shafts have high composite-capitals with a circle of drooping leaves, flower-chalices growing up and two rows of double-volutes with a fluted rectangular unit in-between them.

73 / Square flag of dark stone which once covered the floor

74 / Detail of a tile from Susa.

75 / Detail of the king's baldachin from the Hall of Hundred Columns.

At the top of all this addorsed bull-capitals supported the beams of the ceiling (one well preserved example is to be seen in the Iran-Bastan Museum, see no. 11.5).
Continuing our way through the reception-hall we pass a similar door as in the eastern part on the opposite side and find ourselves in the western portico. This is the side towards the plain, directly above the Terrace walls. In later times the Terrace was enlarged in this part to add two pavilions or porches (fig. 77) which have disappeared by now. Only depressions in the rock give a hint of their existence.
The columns of the western portico are finely decorated, too, but not that elaborate as on the eastern side, because they were supposed to catch one's attention from distance. The bases are covered with large hanging leaves, surrounded by bulges. The middle-ribs are sharply cut and in the upper part covered by smaller leaves with pointed ends above them. Small leaves also fill the gaps at the bottom. A circle of rounded tongues forms the upper border. The capitals were composed from addorsed bulls.
In the northern portico, which had been added later by Xerxes (see chapter 3), the columns are composed of various elements. The bases are similar to those of the western portico, though one can discern a different execution. The leaves are less sharply cut and the lower ends are more rounded. The upper parts of the columns with composite-capitals and addorsed bulls resemble those of the inner hall. In combination with the ornamented bases we have here the richest composition of columns in the whole building. Presumably, in this way Xerxes tried to emphasize his newly created main entrance to the reception-hall.
Two doors lead from the northern portico into the main hall, and these are the only ones in the building which had stone-jambs, obviously, another attempt of Xerxes to emphasize his new main-entrance. Opposite to them, two other doors give access to the store-rooms in the south, which cover the same space as the porticoes on the three other sides.
Great quantities of charcoal were found here, indicating that wooden materials, presumably pieces of furniture, which were needed for the receptions in the hall, must have been stored there. Two exits lead from the store-rooms to the area of Xerxes' Palace (no. 4.7), thus hinting, that this situation should be attributed to Xerxes' building activity.
We continue the round-way through the western portico to the Palace of Darius.

4.4. The Stairway of Artaxerxes III (359/8-338/7 BC) (fig. 76 and 86)

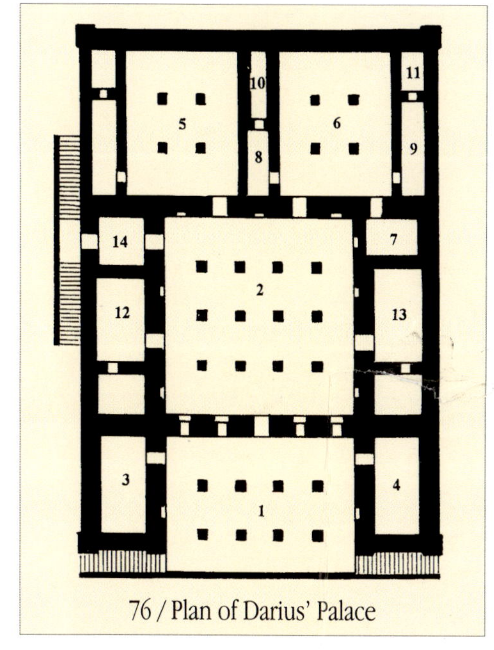

76 / Plan of Darius' Palace

Coming from the western portico of the Apadana one passes first the western side-entrance of the Palace of Darius, whose stairs - according to the inscription - were added by Artaxerxes III. The inscription (A^3Pa) is identical, except for line-division, with the three versions of Palace H (no. 4.6), but it is best preserved on the central panel of this staircase with two flights:

"The Great God is Ahura Mazda, who created this earth, who created yonder sky, who created man, who created happiness for man, who made me, Artaxerxes, king, the one king of many, the one master of many. Proclaims Artaxerxes, the Great King, King of Kings, King of lands on this earth: I am King Artaxerxes' son, Artaxerxes (was) King Darius' son, Darius (was) King Artaxerxes' son, Artaxerxes (was) King Xerxes' son, Xerxes (was) King Darius' son, Darius was the son of Hystaspes by name, of Hystaspes, the son (of) Arsames by name, an Achaemenid.Proclaims Artaxerxes, the King: This stone stairway was built by me in my time. Proclaims Artaxerxes, the King: Me may Ahura Mazda and God Mithra protect and this country and what was made by me!"

77 / Reconstruction of the western facade of the Apadana.

Artaxerxes used elements of the reliefs with subject peoples depicted at the Apadana stairway (see no. 4.3). But his stairs are much smaller, so he could show just a selection and had to arrange them in a different order. Six of them are depicted in three registers on both sides of the central inscription panel. Of the uppermost only the feet and between them the tail of the Ahura Mazda-symbol have been preserved. Others climb up steps above the bull-lion scenes towards the entrance door of the Palace. The internal parapets show servants carrying food upstairs. Their prototypes are to be seen on the southern stairway of the Palace of Darius.

78 / Columns of the Apadana

*4.5. The Palace of Darius (522-486 BC) (fig. 76)

To get a better idea of Darius' Palace one should go further into the courtyard in front of the building and then turn towards its facade. This facade is directed to the south, that means towards the original entrance to the Terrace (see chapter 3). We have to disregard for a moment all those other buildings which are now crowded together on the Terrace thus hiding the Palace of Darius in a remote corner. According to the plan of Darius the visitor entering the Terrace had a free view to the Palace and its facade facing him (fig 80 and 83). To enhance the impression the building was put on a 2,5m high platform. In comparison to the Apadana the Palace seems to be small, but it covers a space of 1160 m^2 The original appearance of the facade can be deduced from the facade of the tomb of king Darius in Naqsh-e Rostam (no. 6.1). Its middle section is a copy of the Palace-facade in exactly the same measurements.

The front of the basement shows rows of guards looking at one another, nine of them at either side of the central panel. They are all clad in the folded court-dresses with long sleeves and wear feather caps. Each holds a lance with both hands, whose apple-shaped knobs again rest on their forward foot (compare the guards on the Apadana stairways, no. 4.3). In addition to the lances they carry bows over their left shoulders and bow-cases on the back. In the centre is an Old Persian inscription (XPc), the Elamite version is on the right and the Babylonian on the left panel, in the back of the guards (fig 96). The same inscription is to be found on the eastern as well as on the western pillar of the portico. It reads:

"*The Great God is Ahura Mazda, who created this earth, who created yonder sky, who created man, who created happiness for man, who made Xerxes king, the one king of many, the one master of many. I am Xerxes, the Great King, King of Kings, King of lands with all kinds of men, King on this great earth far and wide, King Darius' son, an Achaemenid. Proclaims Xerxes, the Great King: By the will of Ahura Mazda this palace was built by Darius the King, who was my father. Me may Ahura Mazda protect together with the gods! And what was made by me and what was made by my father, Darius the King, that also may Ahura Mazda protect together with the gods!*"

Thus we learn, that these inscriptions were added by Xerxes, though he states, that the building was made by his father. The formulation is different from that on the Apadana tiles, where he reports, that he continued the work of his father, and from

79 / Servants stepping up to the platform of Darius' Palace

the inscription on the Apadana stairways (no. 4.3), where he does not mention his father at all. According to the inscriptions of the Palace it is not obvious that Xerxes did add anything else to the Palace-building than these inscriptions.

There are the remains of the representation of winged sun-disk and male sphinxes above the central relief with the inscription-panels as above the exchanged central panel on the Apadana eastern side. The empty spaces are filled with a row of lotus stalks. On both sides the usual scheme of a lion attacking a bull is depicted, framed by rosette borders. The upper one is slanting to the bottom. Above it are indicated steps, which correspond to the real steps behind this parapet. The outer faces as well as the inner flanks of both staircases show rows of servants stepping up to the platform (fig. 79).

They are wearing alternately the court-dresses and the riding-costumes. But both kinds of garment here are combined with a *bashlyk* with which the attendants could cover their mouths so that their breathe would not touch food which they were carrying. They bring covered bowls, skins filled with wine and animals, which still look alive. But this representation must have been chosen to show which different kinds of roast were going to be served to the king and his guests. While stepping up to the portico platform a visitor is accompanied by these servants on both sides. Two rows with four columns each once supported the roof of the portico. The stone-pillars on both sides bear a long inscription (XPc), which is identical to the one on the front of the stairway. The Old Persian is on the top, the Elamite in the centre, the Babylonian at the bottom. The walls which were made of mud-brick have totally disappeared. But they were on a base of courses of stone, the remnants of which are still to be seen. Well preserved are huge stone-blocks of door- and window-frames with fluted cornices.

In some instances windows are made of a single stone though being 2,65 m high, 2,65 m wide and 1,70 m deep. Such a window weighs about 18 tons. The door-frames are put together from monoliths, the entire door weighs about 75 tons. The surface of all these dark stones had been finely polished, thus glittering and appearing almost black. King Darius must have been very proud of these works and he ordered inscriptions *"Frames of stone, made for the Palace of King Darius"* to be written around all the niches and windows, 18 times in all (fig 94). The Old Persian version is in each case on the lintel, the Elamite on the left side running upwards and the Babylonian to the right downwards. The inner door-jambs are adorned with reliefs showing

80 / Darius' Palace reconstructed by Ch. Chipiez

always in one door the same representation but in mirror-reflection. The right and left doors in the portico must have been leading to a guard-room each because two guards with lances are depicted on their jambs. The first of them is holding a high rectangular shield of wicker-work. They all look into the portico and thus seem to protect the entrance to the main hall (fig. 99).

Entering this, one meets the king who is just about to leave the building. He wears a high, crenelated crown. Lateral slots, tiny holes and the rough surface show clearly that once it was covered with a metal-sheet, presumably, gold. Small holes on the king's neck and breast as well as on both sides of his wrists served for fastening necklace and bracelets. Two servants - in smaller scale - follow. One is bearded and holds a parasol above the king's head to protect him from the sun outside the building. The second one, beardless, waves a fly-whisk and carries a towel. Above the reliefs of this main-door there are inscriptions on both sides. The Old Persian version is next to the portico so that it could be read first while entering, then the Elamite and at last the Babylonian version. The inscription reads: "*Darius, the Great King, King of Kings, King of lands, Hystaspes' son, an Achaemenid, who built this palace*" (DPa). So, we can say for certain that this must be the image of king Darius. And by the way, this is the inscription by means of which F. Grotefend could decipher the first Old Persian signs (see chapter 2).

A second trilingual inscription (DPb) was carved on the vertical folds of the king's garment on the western jamb of this doorway: "*Darius, the Great King, Hystaspes' son, the Achaemenid.*" By trying to remove this inscription the dress was badly mutilated. On the corresponding folds on the eastern jamb the excavator E. Herzfeld discovered traces of another inscription in Old Persian and Elamite. But amazingly the name of Xerxes appeared there: "*Xerxes, son of King Darius, an Achaemenid*" (XPk). If this reconstruction is correct, the inscription must have been added, when Xerxes was still crown-prince, because the royal title is omitted. This might suggest that the reliefs in the Palace of Darius were already finished before Xerxes became crown-prince. After his election one of the two representations of King Darius was labelled with the name of the crown-prince, while the Apadana-reliefs were created after that time, thus depicting him standing behind the throne of his father.

The central room of the building (fig. 76,2) had once 3 by 4 columns, now missing. Two doors lead to the north into two rooms with 4 columns each (fig. 76, 5.6). The decoration of both doors is similar. Again the king steps forward (fig. 92).

81 / Xerxes' Palace, relief of servants on the entravce stairway

82 / Relief of the Syrian delegation from the stairway of artaxerxes' I. Plalace

Here too, necklace, bracelets and gold-sheet for the crown had been fixed. A deep triangular cut is under his chin, in which the king's beard in another material, presumably, in lapis lazuli, must have been inlaid. This material was frequently used for beards, and many pieces of such beards were found on the Terrace. A closer look at the garment of the king in the western doorway shows that there are engraved circles with flowers and borders with walking lions (fig. 84). These were sketches for the painters and they help us to get an idea of the richly embroidered dress of the king. The same servants as in the front door follow behind the king. But this time the king is still inside the building and, therefore, he does not need a parasol. So, the bearded servant has put one hand over the other. All the servants who are in the presence of the king and do not hold anything make the same gesture.

The north-eastern room has 5 side-rooms(fig. 76, 7-11)., three of which are directly accessible. A door in the west and one in the east lie on the same axis and their reliefs do notcorrespond to one another but to the reliefs on the opposite door. The southern jambs on both, western and eastern door, depict a servant with an ointment-flask (*alabastron*) and towel who seems to step out of the small side-rooms (fig. 91). On both northern frames - parallel to him - appears a servant with censer (*thymiaterion*) and incense pail containing charcoal.

On either frame of a third door, leading from a small southern room (fig. 76,5) into the same apartment both servants are shown with the same attributes, but now combined. The same two servants appear also in the side-door of the north-western room (fig. 76, 5) which has only two small side-rooms. These rooms in the northern part of the building are badly destroyed and usually not accessible because the remains of the original floor are preserved there. The typical Achaemenid floor is made of a red plaster flooring composed of grains of limestone and calcite covered with red ochre surfacing. When polished it had a dark red shine. One can get an idea of the original appearance of this floor from the restored floor in the museum (no. 4.11). From the central room two doors, to the west and the east respectively, lead to further side-rooms (fig. 76, 12.13). They are adorned with reliefs showing a hero defeating wild beasts. These representations may symbolize the victory over evil powers. The hero wears an Achaemenid court-dress, but to move more easily he has folded up his wide sleeves and thrown them over his shoulder. His long skirt is tucked up and crammed into his belt. He grasps the beast by its forelock on the head or by its horns and thrusts a dagger into its body. Here, again both sides of one door are in the mirror-view so that the hero appears left-handed on one side. The eastern door shows a rampant lion, the western door a lion-griffin-monster with scorpion-tail. These doorways lead into two side-rooms in the west as well as in the east. They are connected with another stone-door showing identical reliefs on both sides. The hero is strangling a young lion with one arm and is holding a dagger in his other hand. On the western side of the main hall there is a second door leading to the side-entrance (fig. 76, 14). There, the hero defeats a bull. But this time he is looking in the opposite direction towards the western entrance which is secured by two soldiers like those in the side-doors of the portico. This proves that already in Darius' time a second entrance must have been here though the preserved stairs were added by Artaxerxes III (see no. 4.4).

With these Palace reliefs, the friezes of the Apadana-staircase and the reliefs of his tomb Darius had created a pictorial program which was copied by his followers again and again.

In all the other buildings of the Terrace we always find the same motifs with only very few alterations. The reliefs of the Palace are directed to somebody who enters the building or stays in the central room. This only makes sense if visitors were indeed allowed to enter the building. Therefore, we can assume, that it functioned as an official building, too, maybe the "office" of the king, from where he was ruling the whole empire.

The two apartments in the northern part may have had more private character where the king could retreat and only few people had access.

According to the plan of Darius the Terrace was the administrative centre of the empire and only official buildings had to be there. His own dwelling-place and that of his family and the members of the court are to be sought at the foot of the Terrace.

In addition there are several inscriptions of later times in Darius' Palace, many of them have historical value. For instance an inscription of AD 311 in Pahlavi (Middle Persian) carved on a door leading to the central room (fig. 76, 2) commemorates a visit and picnic lunch of the Saka king. There Persepolis as a whole is called *satstwny*, "hundred columns", and the Saka king offered blessings to the builder of this Palace. On the opposite site from the entrance to the central room is a beautiful inscription in Nasta'liq from Qajar times (19th c.).

83 / Southern view

f the Darius' Palace

84 / The king's dress, reconstructed by the Tilias from a relief in the Harem

85 / Detail of the king's dress

4.6. The Palace of Artaxerxes I (465-425/4 BC, Palace H) (fig. 97)

There are very few remains of another palace opposite to the Palace of Darius. It was built as a pendant to Darius' Palace, also on a high platform. A mound with some relief fragments indicates the site where the Palace once stood. Rests of the staircase are still to be seen, looking towards the north. An inscription, only in Old-Persian, identical to that one of the western stairs of the Palace of Darius (see no. 4.4) adorns the northern facade three times. Here, Artaxerxes III (359/8-338/7 BC) explicitly says that the staircase was erected by him.

We see extremely long rows of guards, 16 on each side, and, unlike to all other stairways, the steps are not extending behind the facade. Only on the western side steps lead straight up to the podium. These stairs are accompanied by reliefs with subject peoples and servants, comparable to the stairs of Artaxerxes III at the western side of the Palace of Darius (no. 4.4). But here both motifs are mixed and the blocks are in no tectonic connection with the facade.

86 / The stairway of Artaxerxes III at Darius' Palace

87 / Reconstruction of the Darius' Palace by Madam Dieulafoy

They are out of their former context. Other parts are behind the facade of Artaxerxes III or lie in the courtyard, some of them next to the podium of the Palace of Xerxes. A thorough investigation, made by the Tilias (see chapter 1.3), could prove, that in this building two stairways had been reused. Approximately 90 pieces belong to one staircase of black stone, which they were able to reconstruct. Some tiny rests of inscriptions show that these stairs must have been ordered by Artaxerxes I (465-425/4 BC). Thus, A.B. Tilia proposes that Palace H was the original place of the Palace of Artaxerxes I. The site was badly destroyed by fire - as excavations made clear - and were reoccupied in post-Achaemenid times.

88 / 89 / 90 / Views of Darius' Palace at night

91 / Beardless attendant with cosmetic bottle and towel, Darius' Palace

These late inhabitants might have reused better preserved blocks of the stairway of the former Palace. But to improve the facade, they brought the main parts of the stairway of the Palace of Artaxerxes III (no. 4.8) to this site, too. If this assumption is correct, the special execution of the south-western corner of the Terrace could have belonged to the Palace of Artaxerxes I, too. There a parapet of more than 100 pieces found below the Terrace wall could be restored. This parapet shows a singular form. Higher and lower composite elements, crowned by horn-like semi-cones, alternate with each other and are connected by low intermediate elements.

92 / Eastern jamb of northern doorway of the main hall of Darius' Palace. King and two attendants, one of them with flywisk

*4.7. The Palace of Xerxes (486-465 BC) (fig. 98)

Next to the Palace of Darius, joining it at a right angle, lies the Palace of Xerxes. This is a vast complex composed of several buildings on different levels (see no. 4.11, too). For all these Xerxes needed such a lot of space that he had to close the southern entrance and create a new one in the north-west (see chapter 3).
Coming from the courtyard in front of the Palace of Darius a staircase leads up. It is comparable to that of Darius' Palace and also furnished with inscriptions by Xerxes (XPd) in corresponding order. But here he states: "*This palace I built*". The number of guards is reduced to five on each side. The symbol ofAhura Mazda holding the "ring of power" is hovering above the central panel. Smaller stairs leading up to the north-western corner of Xerxes' Palace are composed of reused blocks and may belong to the post-Achaemenid building activities connected with Palace H (see no. 4.6).On the top of the main-stairs a doorway gave access to a smaller courtyard.Presumably, it was flanked byanimal sculptures as rectangular areas at the corners of the stone

93 / Doorways of the Darius' Palace

sill suggest. Buildings are on both sides of the open courtyard and a monumental entrance-gate is on the opposite side. The building to the north is Palace G (see no. 4.8). The one to the south opens with a wide portico with two rows of 6 columns each. The same inscription (XPd) as on the panels of the stairs is carved into both antae. The trilingual inscription (XPe) "*Xerxes, the Great King, King of Kings, King Darius' son, an Achaemenid*" appears on many places in the building. It is to be seen on door and window frames above the reliefs showing the king with his attendants and even on the folds of the king's garment. Stone benches run along all the portico walls. The roof of the main hall was once supported by 36 columns. All these columns have disappeared, just the foundations hewn from the living rock are discernible. But, almost 100 pieces of stone-tori, which must have belonged to this building, have been found on the lower level behind the palace. Most of them are inscribed with Old Persian on the top, Elamite in the middle and Babylonian at the bottom (XPj). Few of them show only the Old Persian version: "*I (am) Xerxes, the*

94 / A cuneiform inscription engraved on one of the doorways of the Darius' Palace

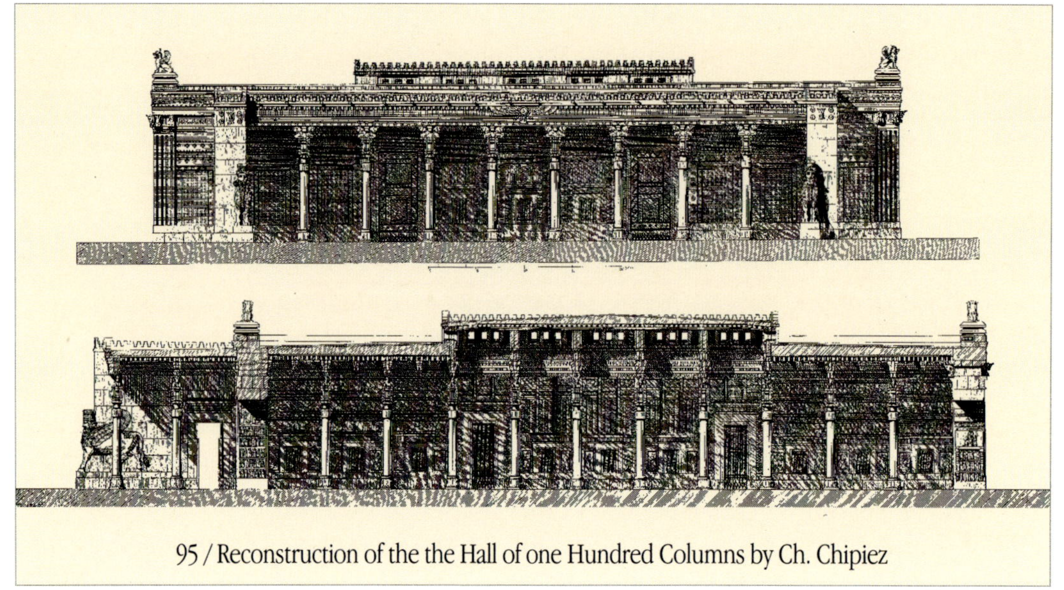

95 / Reconstruction of the the Hall of one Hundred Columns by Ch. Chipiez

Great King, King of Kings, King of lands, King on this earth, King Darius' son, an Achaemenid. Proclaims Xerxes, the King: This palace I have built." Fragments of column shafts and addorsed bull capitals, which must have belonged to the Palace of Xerxes have been found on the lower level of the Harem buildings.

To the right and the left of the main hall there are two rooms which used to have four columns each. These rooms might have had the same functions as the comparable rooms in the northern part of Darius' Palace. On both sides of them are smaller rooms, too. The four stone-doors of the hall are decorated with the image of the king and his servants, copied from the Palace of Darius. Little holes show that they were adorned with jewellery, too. But, it seems strange that also the two side doors depict the king with parasol though he is entering the main hall and not leaving the house. All windows are ornamented with reliefs showing servants. Those from the Darius' Palace with cosmetic bottle and censer appear as well as those from the staircases with wine skins and animals. Small pivot holes in the sills and lintels prove that the windows once had shutters.

The central door in the southern wall has totally disappeared. It gave access to a balcony which is 9,35 m above the level of the Harem-buildings (see no. 4.11 and fig. 113). From there stairs lead up to the eastern and western side of the balcony.

96 / Darius' palace, Xerxes' Babylonian inscription on the facade of southern stairway

Standing on this balcony one looks down on altogether 19 rooms of more or less the same size with four columns each (just two are emphasized by having six columns) and three additional rooms in the south, lying on a lower level on the protruding bastion of the Terrace wall. It has been proposed that all these rooms might have been for the Harem of King Xerxes. They stretch around the corner and were accessible from another monumental building which today houses the Museum (no. 4.11). But the use of all these rooms which are usually called "Harem" is not at all sure.

We return to the open courtyard in front of the central hall. On its eastern side are the remains of an entrance-gate which originally had four columns and a double flight of stairs in front of it, now badly destroyed. They must have looked like the main staircase of the Tripylon (see no. 4.10), which might have been built after this prototype. But, there are nobles stepping up while here servants with food enter the Palace. On the southern wing the Babylonian text of the already known inscription (XPd) is preserved, while its Elamite pendant on the north side is now missing. Two guards on each side flank the Old Persian panel in the centre. Visitors were usually expected to enter from this side. We have to remember that at that time, when Xerxes' Palace was built, the Tripylon did not yet exist. So, this gate was the main entrance to the Palace area. Another open courtyard lies now in front of this gate and to its south are remnants of another big column-hall (no. 4.9).

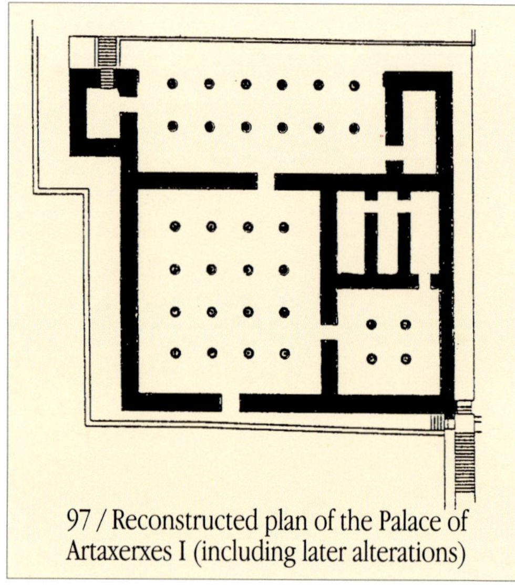

97 / Reconstructed plan of the Palace of Artaxerxes I (including later alterations)

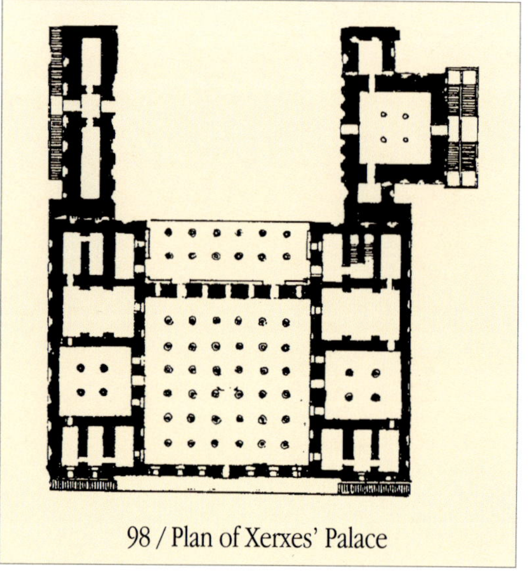

98 / Plan of Xerxes' Palace

99 / Darius' Palace, Persian guards

4.8. The Palace of Artaxerxes III (359/8-338/7 BC, Palace G) (fig. 102)

This building is squeezed in between the southern side of the Apadana and the Palace of Xerxes. The mound is still covered with earth and unexcavated. Therefore, there are no clues to the builder of this Palace. But, because of its somewhat unfortunate situation it must have been built at a time, when the space available on the Terrace was already reduced. Therefore, it might well be assigned to Artaxerxes III. Thus, the reliefs taken in the post-Achaemenid times to the site of Palace H (see no. 4.6) may well have originally adorned the facade of this Palace. Remnants of a stairway depicting servants climbing up steps are still to be seen on the mound.

4.9. The Palace D (fig. 103)

This building lies on the level between Xerxes' Palace and the Harem. The remnants are so scarce that it is difficult to reconstruct even the plan. No attribution to a certain

100 / Xerxes' Palace, western stairway relief, Persian soldiers guarding the stone inscription in Persian

ruler is possible. A L-shaped stone lying south of the eastern entrance to Xerxes'Palace might have served as the pedestal for the nearby found bull statue. Thus, the two bulls which are now in the museum (no. 4.11) might have flanked the entrance of this building.

*4.10. Tripylon (Council Hall) (fig. 107)

This building was, presumably, erected by Artaxerxes I (465-425/4 BC) after he had finished the "Hall of 100 Columns" (no. 4.15) of his father Xerxes. After the construction of the latter the space in front of the Apadana was rather reduced and appeared more corridor-like. So, the Tripylon could combine both buildings and create an architectonic keystone for the eye of a visitor (see fig. 9). Thus, the place got a new unity. On the other hand the building of the Tripylon functioned as a distributor among different sections of buildings, leading from the purely official part with the Apadana and the Hall of 100 Columns to the more restricted parts of the Palaces and - with the third door through a corridor-like side-room downstairs - to the lower

101 / Lion defeating a bull, relief from the Xerxes' Palace stairway

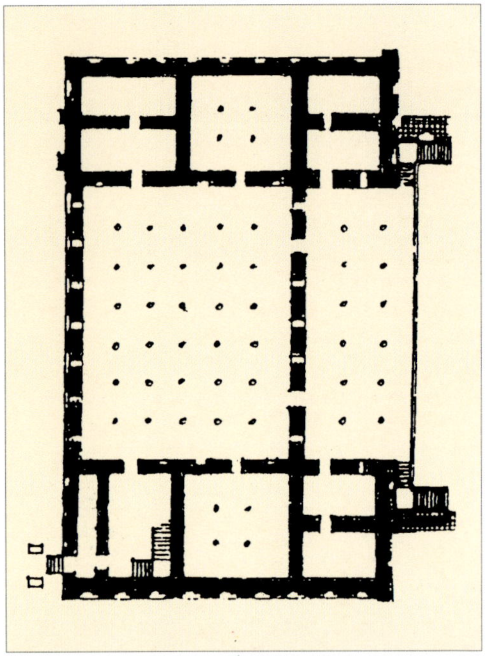

102 / Reconstructed Plan of the Palace of Artaxerxes III

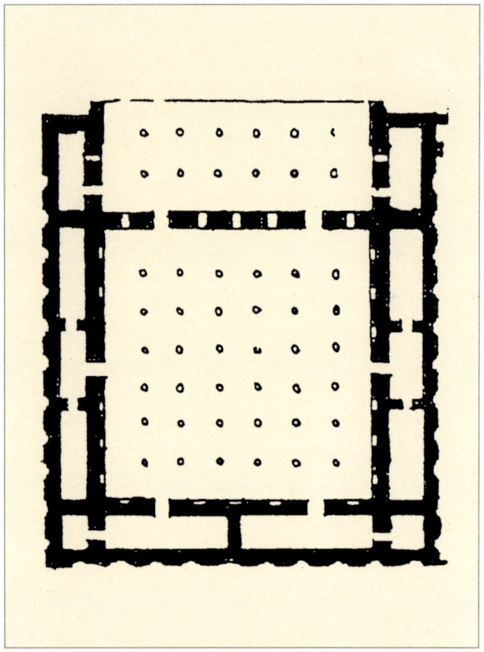

103 / Reconstructed Plan of Palace D

104 / The south-western corner of the Terrace wall

105 / General view of the Xerxes' Palace

106 / Xerxes' Palace, two attendants with an ointment-flask and towel and incense-burner

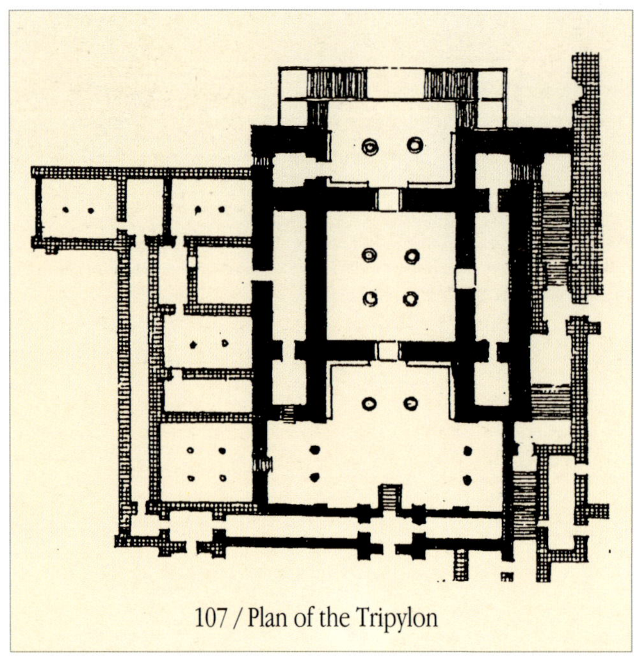
107 / Plan of the Tripylon

108 / Sphinx-capital from the Tripylon

level with the so-called Harem. Because of these three doors it is usually called Tripylon. Its most beautiful facade is the one towards the Apadana. The podium is covered with reliefs showing guards in nearly life-size. The fronts of the lower stairs again show the group of lion and bull on both sides. Long rows of Persian nobles, the prototypes of whom are represented on the Apadana-reliefs in the back of the king, step up the stairs (fig. 150). On the inner side of the landing of the right wing of stairs there is a nice group of two Persians, one of them wearing a crenelated crown. The two columns of the portico - in the north aswell as in the south of the gate-building - had male sphinx-capitals (fig. 108 and 109), remains of which are still to be seen. A better preserved example is in the Museum in Persepolis and another one in the Iran Bastan Museum in Tehran, where it had been transferred, together with the whole staircase of the southern side of the Tripylon, which once lead up to the eastern courtyard in front of the Palace of Xerxes.

109 / Sphinx-capital from the Tripylon, Iran Bastan Museum, Tehran

from the southern doors of the Hall of 100 Columns (no. 4.15). But, in the Tripylon the crown-prince appears again behind the throne of his father. Obviously, Artaxerxes did not have any resentments against this representation. Above all hovers the symbol of the God Ahura Mazda. The traces of colour are still visible and it helped A.B. Tilia in her reconstruction of the former appearance of this symbol (fig. 112).

110 / King and two attendants with towel and parasol from the Tripylon

*4.11. The so-called Harem and Museum (fig. 113)

The main wing of this building is oriented north-south and extends from the Tripylon to the southern wall of the Terrace. To the west another wing extends at the feet of Palace D (no. 4.9) and Xerxes' Palace (no. 4.7). In the south-western corner of the main wing a foundation slab with Old Persian inscription has been discovered (XPf): *"The Great God is Ahura Mazda, who created this earth, who created yonder sky, who created man, who created happiness for man, who made Xerxes king, the one king of many, the one master of many. I am Xerxes, the Great King, King of Kings, King of lands with all kinds of men, King on this great earth far and wide, King Darius' son, an Achaemenid.*

Proclaims Xerxes, the King: My father was Darius, Darius' father was Hystaspes by name, Hystaspes' father was Arsames by name; Hystaspes as well as Arsames were both living, when Ahura Mazda - thus was his will – Darius, who was my father, him he made king on this earth. When Darius became king, much superior he built.

Proclaims Xerxes, the King: Other sons of Darius existed - that was the will of Ahura Mazda -Darius, who was my father, made me the greatest after himself. When my father Darius went away from the throne, by the will of Ahura Mazda I became king in my father's place.

111 / Relief of Ahura Mazda from the Tripylon

When I became king, much superior I built. What had been built by my father, that I took into my care, and other work I enhanced. That also, what I made, and that, what my father made, all that by the will of Ahura Mazda we made. Proclaims Xerxes, the King: Me may Ahura Mazda protect, and my kingdom! And what was made by me, and what was made by my father, that also Ahura Mazda may protect!"

The north-complex of the main wing, adjoining the Tripylon, has been regarded as the quarter of the Harem personnel. The floors of those rooms consisted only of plain stamped earth over a packed stone-and-dirt fill, about 30 cm deep. The eastern stairs of the Tripylon lead directly into this building. Therefore, the question remains, if this part belonged to the original plan of Xerxes' building or was added later on. A well preserved example of a capital with addorsed bulls from the main hall of the Apadana (no. 4.3) is set up in the courtyard.

The columned hall with portico in front of all those similar rooms on the lower level of the Palace-complex of Xerxes, which have been identified as housing for his harem, has been restored and used as museum. In this way, one can get an idea what the buildings looked like before they were destroyed. Especially fine is the polished red floor in the inner hall which is restored according to the original Achaemenid floors. Finely cut bell-shaped bases are preserved but no remnants of columns or capitals have been found. They might have been of wood.

The door reliefs are again copied after those of the Palace of Darius (no. 4.5), and show the king and his servants on the frames of the southern and northern door. They are well preserved, and sketches offlower-motifs and lion-borders are still to be seen on the king's dress (fig. 84). But no jewellery was attached and there are no inscriptions. The jambs of the western doorway show the royal hero defeating a lion, those of the eastern one his fight with a lion-griffin monster with scorpion tail. The portico is flanked by guardrooms with reliefs of two guards on each door jamb.

Exhibits:

Entering the museum one first sees the statue of a dog (fig. 114). It is unfinished, several parts had still to be chiselled away, details of the head and paws as well as the finishing polish are missing (two nicely finished examples of dogs are in the Iran Bastan Museum in Tehran, see no. 11.5). Most entrances of the buildings on the Terrace and in the plain, too, have been adorned with animal sculptures on both

sides, but only in few instances they have been found in situ. -The male sphinx-head in the right-hand corner, coming from the portico of the "Hall of 100 Columns" (no. 4.15), shows how lovely the surface of all the sculptures once was. Here, the polishing is well preserved. - Next to it a cushion-like stone with finely chiselled cuneiform inscription is exhibited. This is the slab with the above mentioned inscription (XPf). The side-room to the right contains some smaller finds from Persepolis. A hole in the floor shows a former floor-level, also covered with the typical Achaemenid red floor. This belonged to the first phase of the Treasury which had been cut off by Xerxes to provide more space for his palace-buildings (see no. 4.13). At the wall to the left is fixed a copy of the Sassanian inscription from Sar Mashhad near Kazerun, which has been written by the High Priest Kartir (compare nos 7.4 and 8.2). In a small room to the south of this side room is a copy of the relief from Pasargadae.
- Between the two southern doors of the main hall there are two examples of bull-statues, nearly life-size, sculptured masterfully (fig. 115).; unfortunately, the heads are missing; one can just discern rests of fine necklaces. They may have belonged to the entrance of Palace D (see no. 4.9).
- Another example of animal-sculpture, a goat or ibex (uncovered together with remnants of a second ibex statue in the vestibule of the northeast tower of the Apadana), can be glanced at through the door to the right of the bulls. That room is not accessible but crowded with objects. Mainly smaller objects found in the Treasury are exhibited in several show-cases.
Coming out of the building to the left a small book-shop is situated in the former guards-room. Below the sill of the westernmost window there are hardly discernible sketches on the stone walls (fig. 122 and 124). Horsemen are represented in atypical Sassanian attire. One of them is wearing a high, rounded cap, ornamented with stars. Ardeshir, the first Sassanian king (224-241) wears a similar one on his coins. Therefore, this sketch and the second one with a standing prince on the southern wall of the eastern side of the portico can be dated to early Sassanian times.
Leaving the museum we turn to the right.On the outer long-side of the building there are corridors in which fragments of the ornamentation of glazed bricks from the Apadana-towers are fixed to the walls (fig. 32). They have lost much of their former splendour but may give an impression of the motifs and colours though they must have been much brighter originally.The remains of the Treasury (no. 4.13) extend parallel to the Museum. Continuing the way between both buildings one reaches a modern staircase about 20 m behind the Museum, which leads down to the southern side of the Terrace walls.

4.12. The southern Wall of the Terrace and Inscriptions

A small protecting roof indicates the place where the inscriptions of Darius are chiselled into the walls in four columns, two of them are Old Persian, one Elamite and one Babylonian. The first column (DPd) reads:

"The great Ahura Mazda, the greatest of the gods, he created Darius, the King, he bestowed the kingship upon him, by the will of Ahura Mazda Darius is king.

Proclaims Darius, the King: This country Persia, which Ahura Mazda bestowed upon me, which is good, with good horses and good men - by the will of Ahura Mazda and of me, Darius, the King, does not fear anybody else.

Proclaims Darius, the King: May Ahura Mazda support me together with 'All Gods', and may Ahura Mazda protect this country from a hostile army, from famine, from Lie. Upon this country may not come a hostile army, nor famine, nor the Lie. I ask for this favour Ahura Mazda together with 'All Gods'. This favour may Ahura Mazda give to me together with 'All Gods'."

112 / The symbol of the god Ahura Mazda from the Tripylon

The second column (DPe) reads:

"I am Darius, the Great King, King of Kings, King of many lands, Hystaspes' son, an Achaemenid.

Proclaims Darius, the King: By the will of Ahura Mazda these are the lands, which I got into my possession with this Persian army, which feared me and to me they brought tribute: Elam, Media, Babylonia, Arabia, Assyria, Egypt, Armenia, Cappadocia, Lydia, the Ionians, who are of the mainland and who (dwell) by the sea, and the lands, which are beyond the sea, Sagartia, Parthia, Drangiana, Aria, Bactria, Sogdiana, Chorasmia, Sattagydia, Arachosia, Sind, Gandara, the Scythians, Maka.

Proclaims Darius, the King: If thus you shall think: 'May I not fear anybody else!', protect this Persian people! If the Persian people shall be protected, the happiness existing very far off, undisturbed – that, too, will come down upon this royal house" (for the peoples mentioned cf fig. 41). In this case the Elamite and Babylonian versions are different. Here should be emphasized just one sentence from the Elamite version, in which Darius states: "*...in former times here did not exist a fortress, by the will of Ahura Mazda I built one, ... and I built it firm and beautiful and strong, so, as I wanted it.*"

These are, presumably, the first inscriptions that were written on the Terrace of Persepolis. And they were close to the first entrance (see chapter 3), whose site is reached after a few steps. There is a recess in the wall, after which

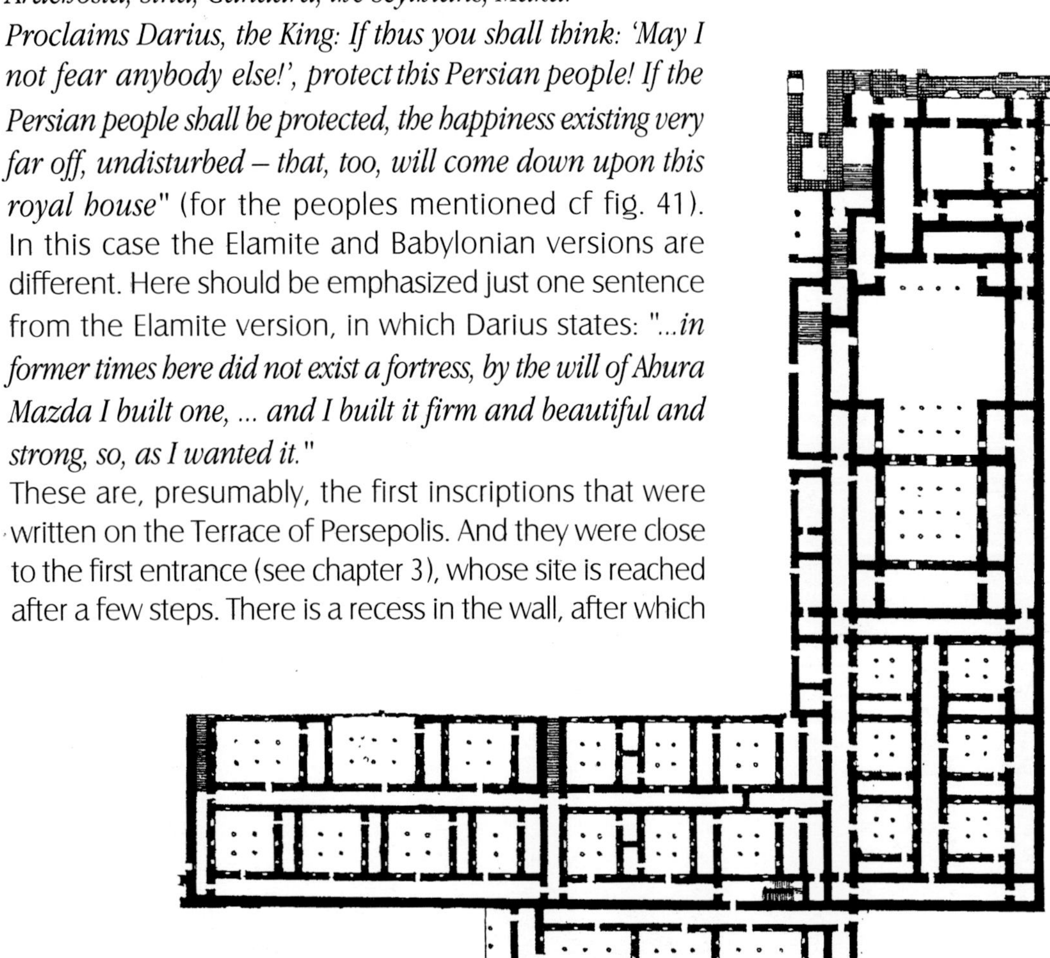

113 / Plan of the so-called Harem-buildings

114 / Dog from Persepolis in the Persepolis Museum

115 /Bull-statue from Persepolis in the Persepolis Museum

116 / Griffin capital, presumably from the Unifinished Gate

117 / A view of the Gate of All Lands at night

118 / Griffin capital

the wall continues to the west.
It is obvious that in this part the stone-blocks of the Terrace-wall are less carefully cut. At a distance of 26 m from the corner there is a clear dividing-line between the roughly cut and reused blocks and the fine masonry of the continuing walls. Investigations on the top of the wall in this area unearthed a recess 7,36 m deep and 18,25 m wide, bordered by neatly cut stones. This clearly indicates the width of the original staircase though it is not possible to say anything about its former shape. Going back the same way at the back corner of the Harem/Museum-building the Treasury is reached to the right.

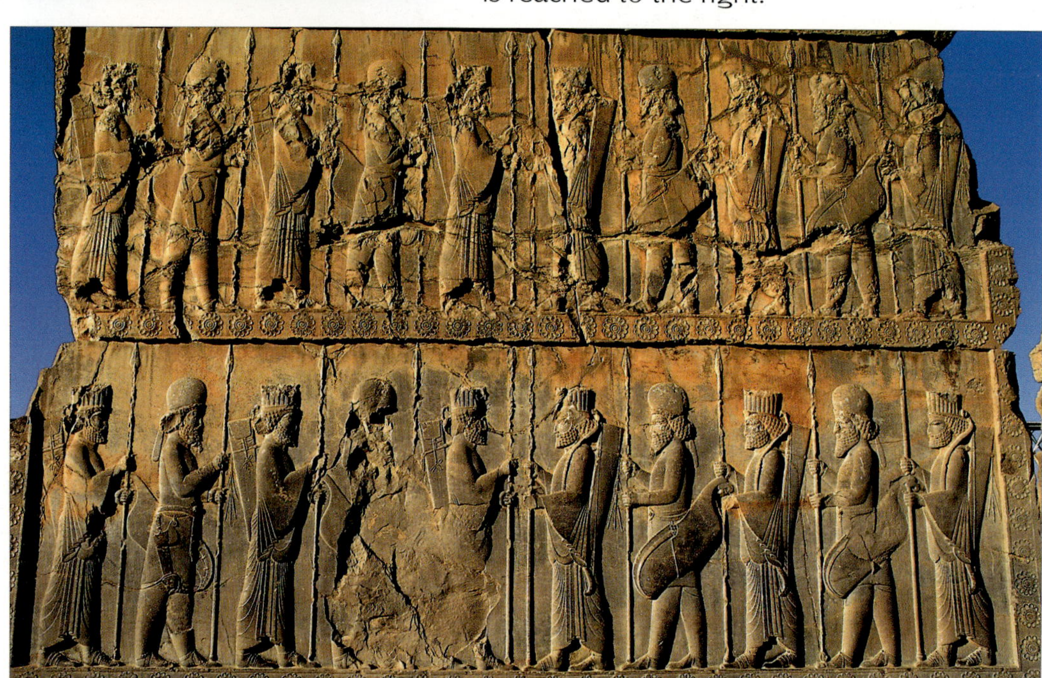
119 / Hall of Hundred Columns (Throne Hall), guards on the north-eastern doorway

120 / Hall of Hundred Columns (Throne Hall), throne-bearers on the south-eastern jamb

122 / Sassanian sketches on the walls of the Harem's portico (after P. Calmeyer and T. Assafi)

123/Apadana eastern stairway, western (inner) face of parapet bordering the central landing, Persian Guards

121 / Hall of Hundred Columns (Throne Hall), guards in the north-western doorway

124 / Sassanian sketches on the walls of the Harem's portico

*4.13. Treasury (fig. 125-128)

The Treasury belonged already to the plan of Darius (see chapter 3). Due to the fact that most public traffic was directed there it was situated next to the original entrance but on a lower level than the representative buildings. When Xerxes started his building activities on the Terrace the Treasury suffered, too. It was cut off in its western parts and was enlarged towards the north. But the excavators under E.F. Schmidt were able to reconstruct the lost parts. A piece of the former floor is still to be seen in the Harem/Museum-building (see no. 4.11). Altogether three building-phases can be discerned.

1st Phase (fig. 128)

From outside the Treasury looked like a castle. Thick mud brick-walls, once about 11 m high and without any windows, enclosed the whole building (120,70 by 61,90 m). All along the walls of the building there were small elongated rooms with thick walls at their inner side, too, thus providing altogether an immensely stabile enclosure for the large rooms, in which the valuables were kept. The outer facade was divided

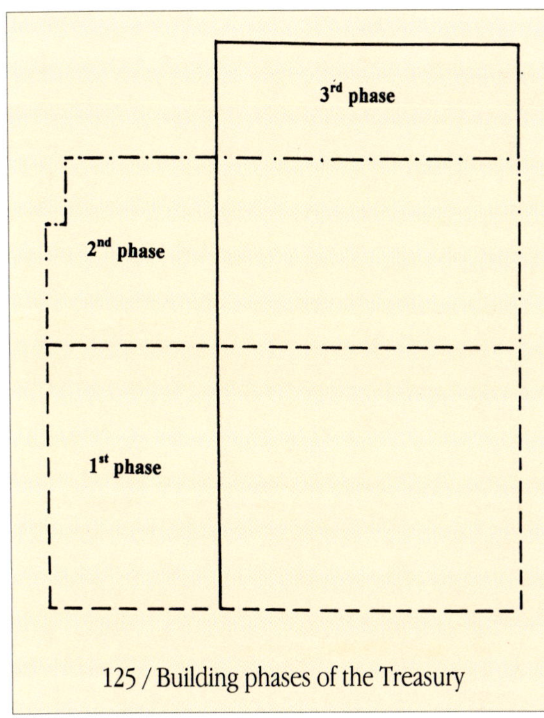

125 / Building phases of the Treasury

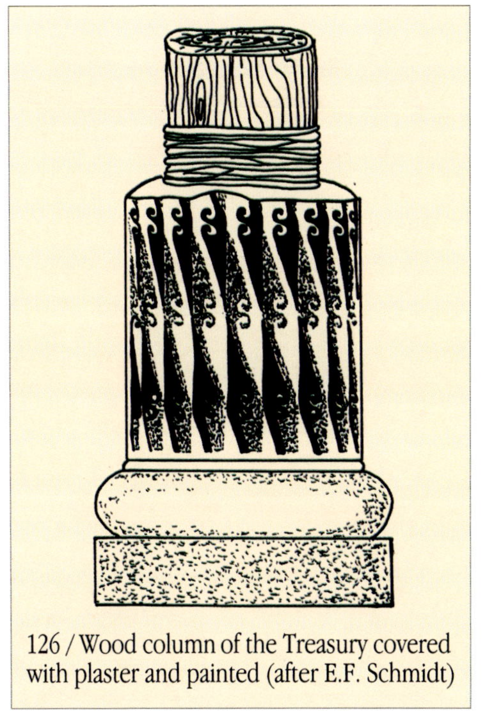

126 / Wood column of the Treasury covered with plaster and painted (after E.F. Schmidt)

into stepped niches and protruding pillars, each 2 m wide. The pillars were adorned with arrow-like slots. Thus the building had a massive but not too strange appearance. The entrance to the Treasury lay in the west, next to the original entrance to the Terrace. One first entered a small room (fig. 128,1), presumably, for guards who had to control the arriving person. After that a second door led into a corridor with two rooms of the same size to the right and to the left, with four columns in each (fig. 128,2.3).

All columns in the Treasury were made of wood, except for the stone bases. To construct the columns wicker was wound around 35-40 cm thick stems of trees and then covered with a layer of mud 8-10 cm thick. Thus, the columns reached a diameter of about 60 cm and were coloured with white, red and blue. Only few remains of those columns have been found, but enough to restore their former appearance (fig. 126). We may assume that these two rooms were the offices of those functionaries who had to deal with the public. Here, the messengers arrived with letters and accounts from all over Persis. Shipments with tributes and taxes of various kinds arrived here. They had first to be controlled and booked before they

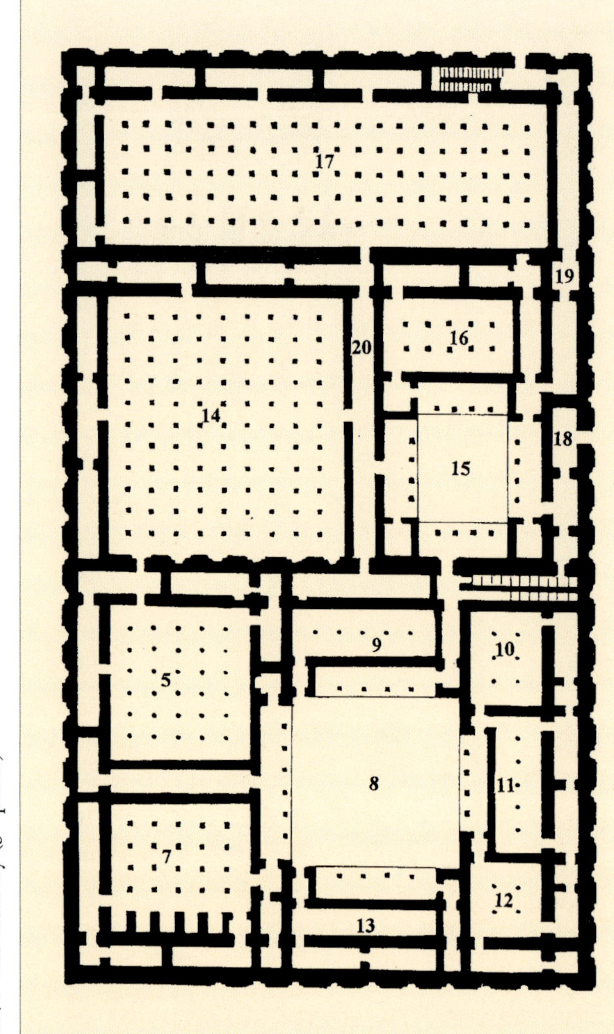

127 / The Treasury (3rd phase)

were deposited in the Treasury. Large rooms to the right and left of the long corridor, presumably, served for depositing. Those to the north (fig. 128, 4.5) had 36 columns each, those to the south (fig. 128, 6.7) only 24 but in addition deep niches for shelves. As we can imagine, the latter ones were packed with precious vessels of silver, gold or glass, or clothes embroidered with gold-wire and pearls. It was not possible to get into those storerooms directly from the corridor. One had to enter first the inner courtyard with porticoes on all four sides (fig. 128.8) and then pass through another small room on either side of the western portico, surely with another control. Presumably, only very few people were allowed to enter the inner courtyard. Large rooms behind the remaining three other porticoes may have been the seat of central administration. The doors were made of wood and adorned with bronze-sheets. Fabulous creatures and bands with rosettes, partly gilded, must have been fixed on them, because many tiny pieces, especially fragments of wings, have been found everywhere in the Treasury.

The eastern portico like the western one has two small rooms on either side. The northern one gives access to two rooms. The most spacious one (fig. 128,10) with six columns covering 140 m^2 is directly to the north. In the background a door leads to two small adjoining rooms. From the same antechamber a large room in the east (fig. 128,11) is accessible.It shows a row of five columns and again two small side-rooms. The southern room (fig. 128,12) with its own antechamber is more or less square with four columns and two doors leading into side-rooms. Thus, we have here an assembly of three spacious roomswhich are separated but also easily reached from each other.

These may have been the offices of the highest functionaries, the marshal of the royal household in the largest room in the north, his vice-marshal in the south and between them the royal chancellery. The side-rooms could have been used for storing tablets, i.e. the current archive.

Further storage-place was in the rooms to the south of the courtyard where impressions in the floor might stem from wooden shelves which had been fixed on the walls. Another five columned large room(fig. 128,9) with separate entrance-room and side-rooms, too, is to the north of the courtyard. The seat of the treasurer might have been in it. So we can imagine that the most important functionaries of the administration had their seats around this courtyard in the Treasury.

The eastern door of the northern portico leads into a corridor and then to two ramps in the corner of the building which gave access to either the roof or a second storey.

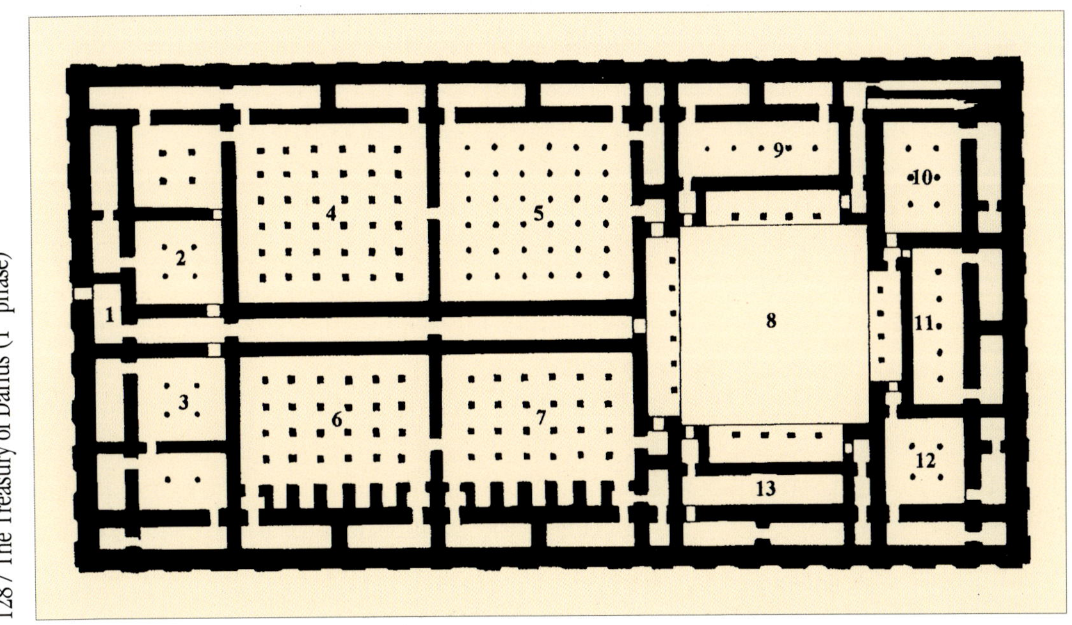

128 / The Treasury of Darius (1st phase)

2nd Phase

Still under the reign of Darius the Treasury was enlarged towards the north to nearly twice its former size. A large hall with 121 columns was added of which after the alterations of Xerxes still 99 remained (fig. 127, 14). In addition asecond courtyard (fig. 127, 15) with a large room with ten columns to its north was built (fig. 127, 16). This room again could be entered only through a small antechamber. It seems that the treasurer needed more space for his office and therefore was moved to the new building. And in this very room the tablets have been found which are called Treasury-tablets after their finding-place. They deal with payments in silver for the workers ordered by the treasurer. These tablets had collapsed during the fire from an upper room where they had been stored. So, in this case we can be sure that, at least, in this part of the building a second storey had existed. Because of the fire the tablets were accidentally burned and, thus, survived until our days. Most of the administration tablets were just dried in the sun and therefore disappeared like all the mudbrick-walls.

3rd Phase (fig. 127 and 140)

As has been said (see chapter 3) the whole appearance of the Terrace was changed under Xerxes. The western parts of the Treasury were cut off to give room for his new Harem-buildings. As substitution for the lost space he added another large hall to the north (fig. 127, 17). Just a small street separates the Treasury from the Harem-buildings in the west and the Hall of 100 Columns to the north, but there are no entrances to the Treasury from those sides. But also the former entrance from the west was cut off and a new entrance created at the eastern side of the building (fig. 127, 18). Now all those who had to go to the Treasury entered through a heavily fortified entrance at the south-east. This must have been also the entrance for all the services. The new eastern entrance to the Treasury led again through a guards- and control-room. Through another room one could enter the courtyard. This courtyard became now the representative centre of the new Treasury.

The central reliefs of the Apadana staircases were brought into the eastern and southern porticoes. The original one from the east of the Apadana is still to be seen there (see no. 4.14), while that one from the northern stairs is now in the Iran Bastan Museum in Tehran (see no. 11.1). In front of the central door of the western portico and the northern door of the eastern portico animal statues were set up at both sides of the doors.

Just the impressions of their bases have been preserved which show that they must have been life-size and we can imagine their appearance due to the examples in the Museum (see no. 4.11). The doors themselves were richly decorated. Remains of painted ornaments were found here. The doors were framed by bright blue bands with a red stripe with white rosettes with a blue centre.

Of all the valuables which were stored in the large Treasury halls only few pieces have been left.The contents were thoroughly robbed by the soldiers of Alexander the Great in 330 BC and by generations of treasure hunters who came after them. But, in the northern parts of the Treasury, which were covered with thicker layers of destruction material and collapsed mud brick-walls, the excavators managed to find several pieces which can give us a hint about various kinds of treasures that had been stored there. Some of those objects are exhibited in the Persepolis Museum (see no. 4.11), but more representative examples are in the Iran Bastan Museum in Tehran (see no. 11.4). Not only the large halls were filled with all those things, but also the corridors and in the late Achaemenid times the porticoes of the first building were closed with walls and served as storage rooms, too. In that time the administration must have been located somewhere else. They either moved to another building or maybe upstairs to the second floor. The existence of the upper storey is suggested by stairs in the northern wall leading up and the remains of collapsed walls and smaller column-bases (with a diameter of 41-42 cm).

4.14. The "Treasury-relief"

One of the most important examples of early Achaemenid art is still to be seen unprotected in the open air (fig. 129 ff.). It is usually called "Treasury-relief" after its finding-place in the Treasury. Only during the restoration works executed in the 60-70's the Italian architects, the Tilias, could find out the original location of this relief and its pendant, now in the Iran Bastan Museum in Tehran (no. 11.1). The piece in Persepolis was the centre of the eastern staircase of the Apadana. Thus, it belongs to the original plan of king Darius (522-486 BC) and this is exactly the piece that fits into the program (see chapter 3 and no. 4.3). The king looks to the left, that means - at its original place - towards the arriving subject peoples on the reliefs and likewise towards every person that arrived on the Terrace from the original entrance in the south. The king is sitting on a throne, his feet on a stool (fig. 130). His importance is shown by his size. Though he is sitting he is depicted larger than all the other

130 / King Darius on his throne

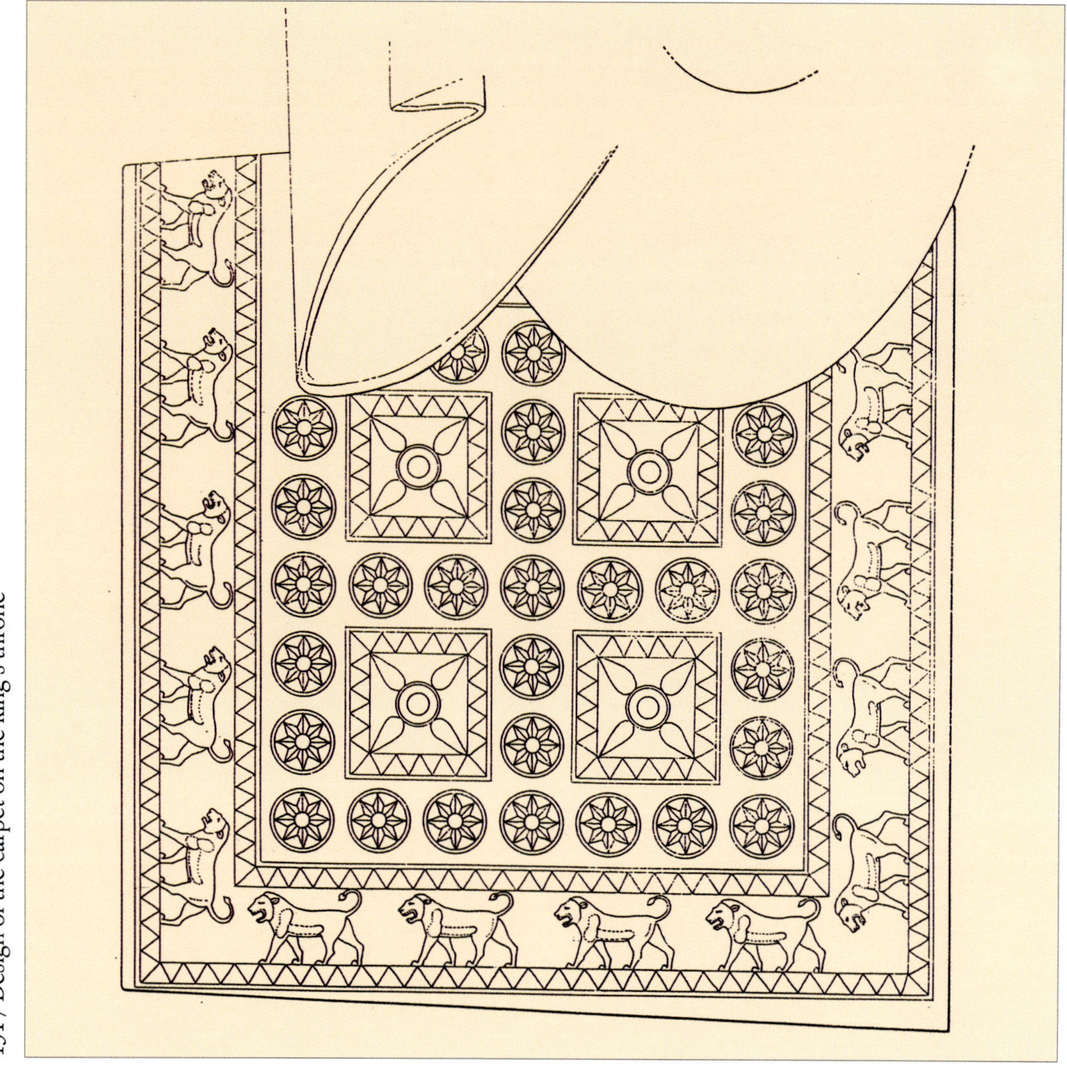
131 / Design of the carpet on the king's throne

persons on the relief. His hair is done in the typical Achaemenid way with well executed tiny curl-locks. His long beard is coiffured after the fashion of the old Assyrian kings with alternating rows of curls and wavy hair. Only the king and the crown-prince were allowed to wear such a long beard. The high cap which looks now plain must have been richly ornamented. On the reliefs in the Palace of Darius (no. 4.5) they were originally covered with gold-sheets. Maybe here this was only indicated in painting. For we have to remember, that this relief too, like all the others,

132 / The king's guards on the "Treasury-relief" (detail of fig. 129)

133 / The King's chamberlain and weapon- bearer on the " Treasury relief "

134 / „Treasury relief", detail of the two incense-burners

135 / A silver censer like those on the „Treasury relief"

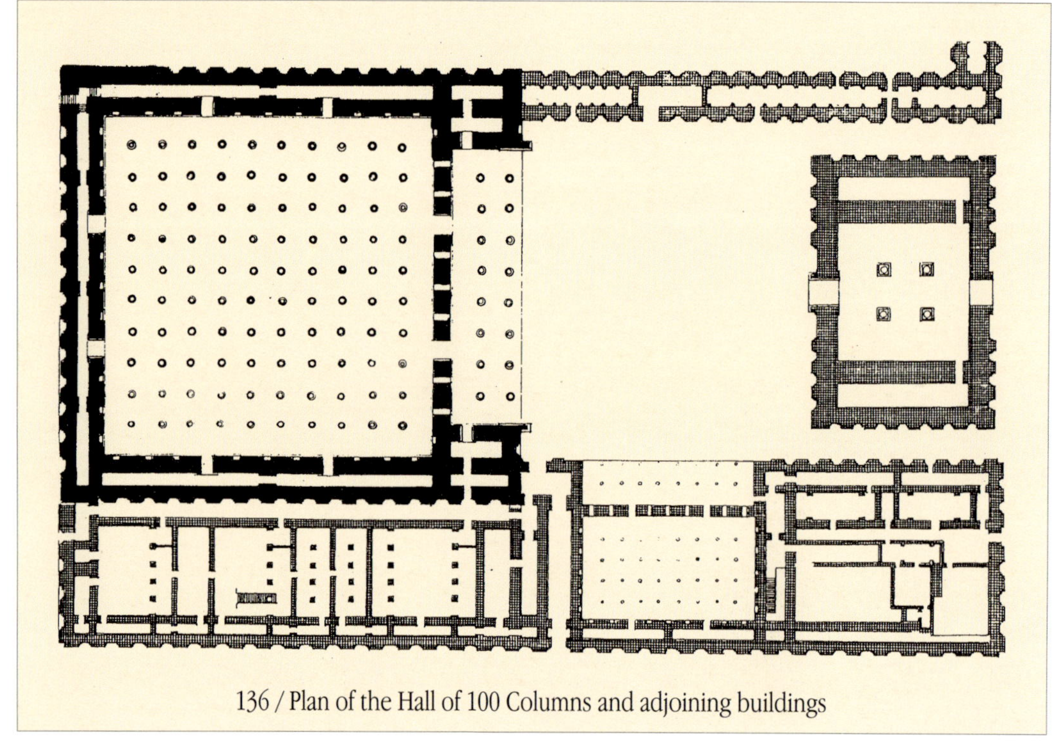

136 / Plan of the Hall of 100 Columns and adjoining buildings

137 / „Treasury relief “, detail of King Darius holding a lotus flower

138 / „Treasury relief “, detail of a servant holding a bucket which may contain charcoal for the incense-burners

139 / Tripylon (Council Hall), a Persian guard on the eastern facade of the southern stairway

once was painted in bright colours. The king wears the Persian court-dress with its wide sleeves. His dress must have been ornamented with two different types of flowers in the circles and borders of walking lions, whose sketches are still to be seen on the reliefs in the Palaces and the so-called Harem (see no. 4.5, 4.7, 4.11). The shoes of the king must have been of very soft leather so that he could slip in without needing straps. Only the king and the crown-prince are wearing these fine shoes. In his right hand the king is holding a sceptre with a knob on its upper end, presumably, all made of gold. In his left hand he is holding a lotus-flower with two buds. Again, only the king and the crown-prince are holding flowers with two additional buds.

The throne of the king is finely executed and its legs seem to be well-lathed. The feet end in lion-paws while those of the stool are rendered as bull-hoes. This must have a special symbolic meaning and may refer to the lion-bull combats which so often appear in the relief program. The animal-feet of the furniture don't touch the floor but are set on further feet ornamented with drooping leaves. Traces of paint show that the leaves were alternating red and blue thus indicating that the original was inlaid with carnelian and lapis lazuli. The king sits on a cushion under which a rectangular piece like a blanket is visible. Traces of painted ornaments which were found by the Tilias on the representation of the king in the Hall of 100 Columns have shown that this must have been a carpet (fig. 131). Its ornamentation is comparable to an original Achaemenid carpet which was found in a frozen tomb in Pazyryk in Siberia.

The crown-prince is standing behind the throne of his father, in reality, presumably, to his side (fig. 129). Though he is standing he is not taller than his seated father, but on the other hand he towers above all other persons. Unfortunately, the image of the crown-prince is much destroyed here (better preserved is Xerxes' copy from the northern stairs, now in Tehran [no. 11.1]; see this also for the restoration of the two following persons). His clothing is like that of the king.

Next follows the chamberlain. He wears the Achaemenid court-dress but combined with a bashlyk which would match the riding-costume. It seems that all the servants who had direct access to the king had to wear bashlyks to be able to cover their mouths not to molest the king with their breath. The chamberlain has put his right hand over the left, a gesture which we have already seen on the reliefs in the Palace of Darius (no. 4.5), and holds a towel. He is unbearded and might therefore have been either very young or an eunuch.

The king's weapon-bearer is clad in the Iranian riding-costume, combined with the round felt-cap. Over his right shoulder he carries the king's bow-case *(gorytos)* and holds his battle-axe in the left hand. Both, the battle-axe and the short sword (*akinakes*), hanging to the right side of his body and, therefore, not visible, are extremely finely executed in the mirror-image which is now in Tehran (no. 11.1). The post of the baldachin with the lower tassels of its sky which covers the whole scene is to be seen in the back of the weapon-bearer. Two blocks of the sky with rows of lions walking from both sides towards the winged sun in the middle were found reused for the steps of Palace G (no. 4.8). Outside the baldachin two guards are standing (fig. 132), the first holding a lance, the second an upright flag. The painted motif has now disappeared from the rectangular flag. From the left the king is approached by a man in Iranian riding-costume wearing the rounded cap with animal-tail (fig. 129). He bends forward and covers his mouth with his hand, because he does not want to molest the king with his breath, though there are still two incense-burners separating the two of them. They are very finely executed. Original comparable pieces have been found(fig. 134 and 135). The high stands are fluted in the typical Achaemenid way, with drooping leaves on the top. The bowls which contain the charcoal and incense have high conoid covers with arrow-like slots. A small lotus-flower is at the top of both. Long chains of the covers, executed in different ways, are fixed to the stands by small ducks' heads, so that the covers can't get lost. The man who is approaching them might be the king's marshal, the highest official after the king, who was Farnaka for many years during Darius' reign. Still in Safavid times a silver-staff was the badge of this rank. His high position is also shown by his large ear-rings with pendant. We can imagine that he is just announcing to his majesty that the representatives of all the subject peoples had arrived to offer their gifts. To the left, outside the baldachin, another lance-bearer is standing as a pendant to the right one. And a servant, with one hand put above the other, holds a bucket which may contain charcoal for the incense-burners. The whole scene is framed by bands ornamented with rosettes.

140 / On the left Harem of Xerxes, western and southern facades of the main wing, restored, with the excavated Treasury in the foreground

*4.15. The Hall of 100 Columns (Throne Hall) (fig. 136 and 141)

Coming from the Treasury one enters the building from its backside. This building was planned by Xerxes (486-465 BC) and finished by his son Artaxerxes I (465-424 BC). A foundation record has been found in the south-eastern corner of the main hall (only Babylonian version): "*Proclaims Artaxerxes the King: This house Xerxes the King, my father, laid its foundations in the protection of Ahura Mazda; I, Artaxerxes the King, built and brought (it) to completion*". It is uncertain if there did exist a need for this new hall or if Xerxes just wanted to create a beautiful building that could compete with the Apadana, the reception-hall built by his father. The space on the Terrace was limited by now. Thus, he restricted the porticoes to just one on the northern side, towards the new entrance (see chapter 3). The portico is flanked on both sides by walls adorned with huge bulls (the head of the eastern one is now in the Oriental Institute Museum, Chicago), which are otherwise only known in the architecture of gates. In this case both types are combined in one. The capitals of the portico columns (2 by 8) had the shape of addorsed human-headed bulls (confer those of

141 / The Hall of 100 Columns seen from the Northern Tomb; in the background the Apadana and further back to the left Darius' Palace

142 / Reconstruction of the Hall of Hundred Columns by Ch. Chipiez

the Tripylon, no. 4.10), as could be reconstructed only by scattered fragments. Two bronze-sheets ornamented with rosettes and 21 gold-capped nails were found in the portico. One would expect that they once were attached to wooden doors but no pivoting devices have been found. Light fell into the hall through seven windows in the portico. The other walls show only niches, nine in each. The new hall covers a space of 4700 m² (68,5 m square, while the Apadana has 3660,25 m²). A visitor who was allowed to enter it must have been puzzled by the 100 columns, which gave the building its name. The hall presumably seemed endless, but the columns are less finely executed with only 36 flutes. Their height was 12,96 m, that of the Apadana columns 19,10 to 19,27 m. The two doors in the east and the west are decorated with combat-scenes of a royal hero with beasts which were copied after the reliefs in the Palace of Darius (see no. 4.5), but in a much larger scale. In the northern doorway the fight with composite monsters is depicted on both sides. In the southern ones the fight with the lion and the bull are rendered respectively. Exceptional is the beaked monster in the northern door of the western wall. It shows the same mixture of bird and lion as the ornaments of the king's sword from the central panel of the northern side of the Apadana (now in the Iran Bastan Museum, no. 11.1). But these doors - as well as the southern ones - lead only into passages which encompass the building on three sides. On the eastern side they are divided into two separate rooms. So the reliefs are mere adornments of the

143 / Hall of Hundred Columns (Throne Hall), bull from the eastern side of the portico

inner hall. The entrance-doors from the north are emphasized. The central scene of the Apadana-stairs with the king on his throne and the marshal of the royal household approaching him (see no. 4.14) appears on the upper part. But instead of the crown-prince the chamberlain is represented immediately behind the throne, carrying the towel and in addition a fly-whisk. This rendering gives us a hint that it was indeed Xerxes who removed the central panels from the stairs (see chapter 3). Below the throne royal guards are rendered in five registers. This representation is repeated four times, on all the northern door-frames, always directed towards the arriving visitor. The throne-motif is also to be found on the southern doors but shortened. Only the king and the servant with the fly-whisk are represented there (fig. 147). But, this time the king is sitting on a stage which is supported by the peoples of the empire, a motif that occurred first on the Tomb of Darius (see no. 6.1). Because the space on the door-jambs was limited, here the representatives of the peoples are divided on the eastern and western jambs. The reliefs are directed towards the inner hall, no visitor was supposed to pass these doors. Only the king and the servants may have had the possibility to slip out from here through a small door directly into the quarters of the palaces.

4.16. Rooms in the East of the Hall of 100 Columns and the Tunnel (fig. 136)

In the east of the open courtyard in front of the Hall of 100 Columns lies a portico with two rows of eight columns. Parts of three of the addorsed bull capitals are preserved. Two doors lead into a spacious room with 4 by 8 columns. Several of the nicely shaped bases are still in situ. To the north and south of this hall adjoin complexes with smaller rooms. In the east of the Hall of 100 Columns a well wrought staircase descends to atunnel system. It is cut into the rocks, 1,75 to 2,10m high and an average width of 1,15 m (fig. 146). Thus, servants could enter to clean the tunnels.The top of the tunnel is about 1,5 m below the lowest floor level.

*4.17. The so-called Unfinished Gate (fig. 136)

In the late Achaemenid times a huge gateway, which was never finished, was started to be built in front of the Hall of 100 Columns. Its direction is towards the hall and it might have been planned in connection with the erection of the mud brick-wall, which is dividing the space north and east of the Apadana from the Hall of 100 Columns.

144 / Palace of Darius, northern jamb, southern doorway in western wall, hero's combat with a horned lion-headed monster

Though the gate is not finished it is interesting to see the different phases of its manufacture. Huge blocks were put one onto the other and at their final location the finer execution of the bulls was started(fig. 248 and 149). An already finished column -base was put together with the first drum. But this was left in a rather rough state, only the part which had to fit directly onto the base had been already smoothed. On all four sides of the base there are different signs, arrow-like (fig. 145) or a ring on a stick, which correspond to the same signs on the drum. These were masons' marks to know exactly where to join one piece with another. Usually, those signs were removed after finishing and were no longer to be seen. The finely executed addorsed bulls capital, lying next to the Unfinished Gate, belong to the Apadana-hall.

4.18. The Griffin-capitals (fig. 116 and 118)

In two smaller rooms north of the way back to the Gateway of all Lands (no. 4.1) two griffin-capitals in exquisite finishing are exhibited. These are the only ones of this kind. It is assumed, that they have been prepared for the Unfinished Gate (no. 4.17).

145 / Mason's marks on torus and drum of a column from the Unfinished Gate

146 / The Tunnel

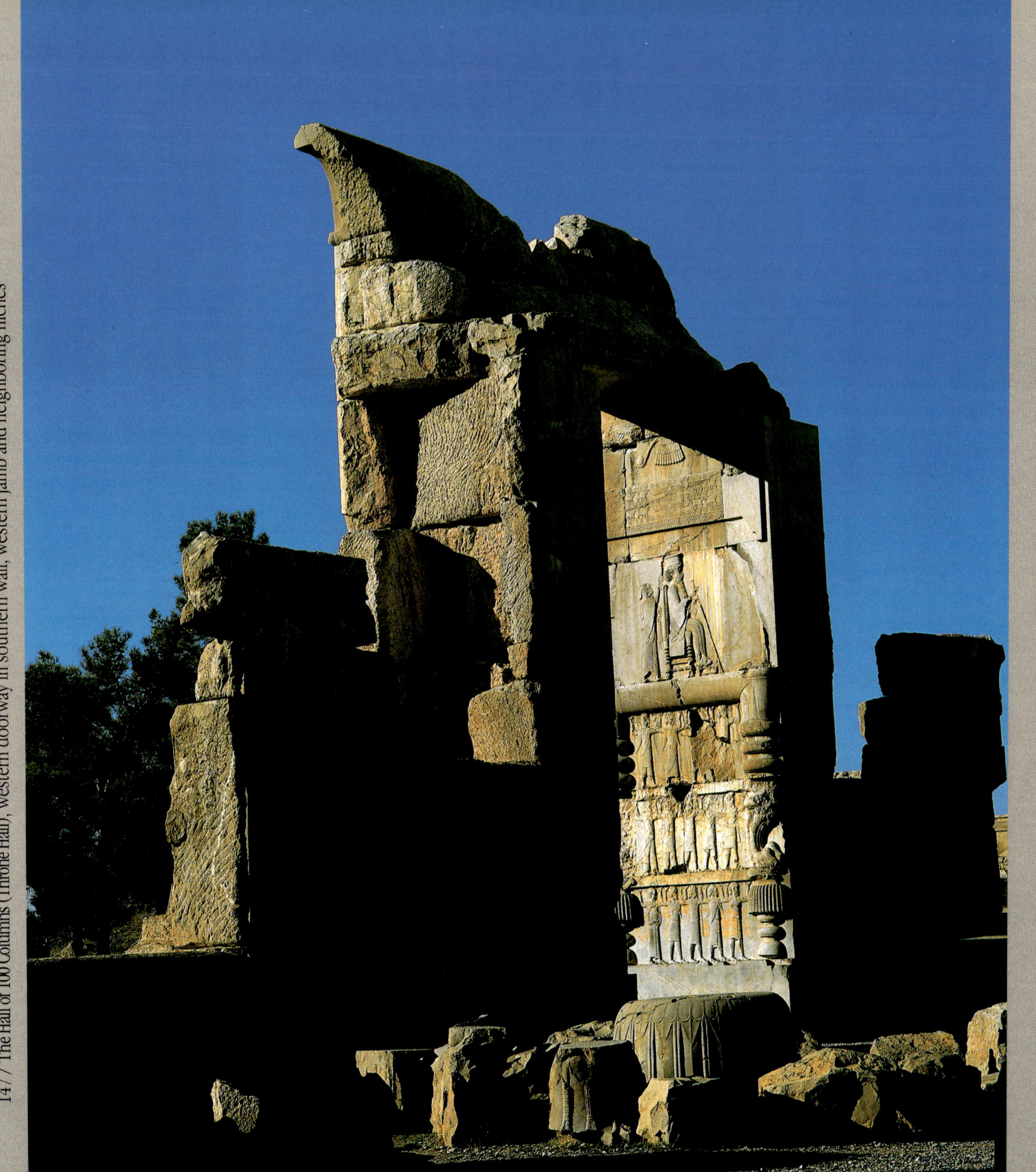

147 / The Hall of 100 Columns (Throne Hall), western doorway in southern wall, western jamb and neighboring niches

4.19. Northern Tomb, presumably of Artaxerxes III (359/8-338/7 BC) (Tomb VI)

From the Unfinished Gate one may follow a small footpath leading up to the first tomb to the north. The view from there is terrific with the entire Terrace and all the buildings at one's feet. Looking down, to the right the northern fortification-wall climbs up the mountain-slope. It encloses the top of the hill. On that upper level there are also remains of various buildings but they are badly preserved and not yet closely studied.

The tomb is a copy of Darius' one in Naqsh-e Rostam (see no. 6.1). Three of his successors copied this design for their own tombs on the rocks of that site. But, no inscription was added. So, the tombs cannot be attributed with certainty. The late Achaemenid kings transferred the same kind of rock-tombs to the Kuh-e Rahmat in the back of the Terrace of Persepolis. Only the southern one shows inscriptions (see no. 4.22). For the description see the Tomb of Darius in Naqsh-e Rostam (no 6.1). But the lower plain part is omitted because the rock is not that high as in Naqsh-e Rostam. Here a visitor may have a closer look, standing in front of the relief. The facade of Darius' Palace with its entrance-door in the middle and the columns of the portico, which are lost in the original building, appear again. But the length of

148 / The Unfinished Gate

the facade exceeds that of the Palace by 1,6 m while the vertical dimensions are very close. The capitals were composed of bulls and their horns were fixed separately. They may have been of another material, for instance gilded bronze. A new addition is the lion-frieze on the entablature. Another dissimilarity from the Tomb of Darius are three rows of pairs of guards on the side walls. But, on the other hand the cornice above the door shows 24 flutes, that one of Darius' Palace 26, while the earlier tombs are rather ill-proportioned with more than 35 flutes. The proportions of the figures on this relief look much clumsier than on the original, thus indicating a rather late manufacture, too.

The sepulchral compartments consist of a vestibule parallel to the facade, slanting to its left side (like Tomb no. 6.3 in Naqsh-e Rostam). Three vaults contain two stone coffins each. The stone lids are flat at the bottom and semi-elliptically rounded on the top. It is not sure, if the tomb facade was to be seen from the Terrace, because remains of a building are in front of the tomb. This building corresponds in orientation with those on the Terrace - not with the tomb (21° difference). The purpose of this is not known. Were there guards to protect the tomb? Or was it indeed intended to hide the tomb? It was separated from the Terrace by a fortification-wall. But the ground in front of the tomb was about 7 m higher than the parapet of the fortress. A gate in the middle, strengthened by two towers (at least 11,5 m high), gave access to the tomb and the cistern. A trench on the eastern side of the wall, 6 to 9,5 m wide at the bottom, served two purposes. It helped to protect the Terrace platform not only from enemies but also from the floods of heavy winter rains.

149 / The Unfinished Gate

One may continue the footpath on the slope of the mountain towards the south.

150 / Tripylon (Council Hall), Persian dignitaries on southern wall of the upper flight of eastern wing of the main stairway

4.20. The Rock-cistern

An enormous cistern (4,15 m square) is cut deep into the rock. It has been excavated to a depth of 24 m without finding a lateral tunnel or reaching the shaft bottom. The latter must, therefore, lie below the base of the Terrace foundation. Rain-waters flowing down from the mountain were gathered in several channels. The cistern was, presumably, covered by planks. Rock-cuttings for three enormous beams are still to be seen. There is a level space cut out of the rocky slope (2,6 by 6,15 m) on the eastern side. In its south-eastern corner it is connected with a canal, once covered with stone slabs. The way continues to the next tomb in the south.

4.21. The so-called Garrison-quarters

While following the foot-path to the south one looks down on the various halls of the Treasury (no. 4.13). To the east of it runs a small road which led to the entrance of the Treasury and further on to the buildings next to the Hall of 100 Columns (no. 4.15). It might have served for providing supplies. Poorly preserved

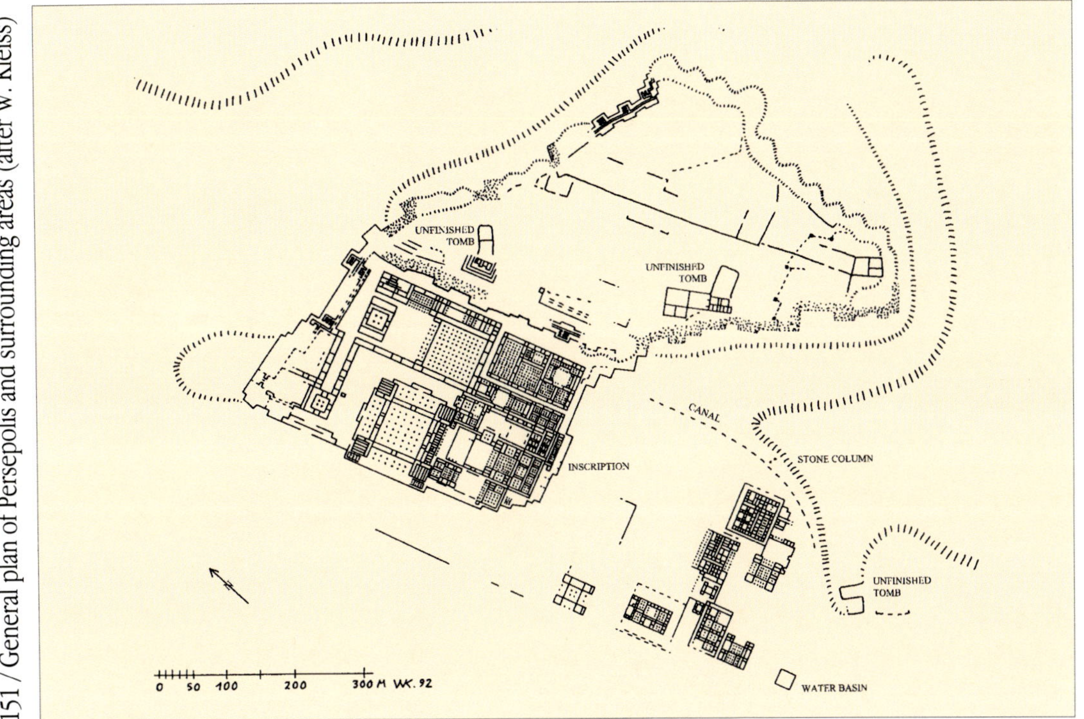

151 / General plan of Persepolis and surrounding areas (after W. Kleiss)

remnants of mud brick- walls are leaned against the remains of the eastern fortification wall and the mentioned road. Sherds of rather plain table ware and some arrow points have been found in the rooms. Due to these finds and the situation next to the fortification wall they are called Garrison-quarters.

4.22. The Southern Tomb, presumably of Artaxerxes II (405/4-359/8) (Tomb V)

This tomb is situated about 250 m east-south-east of the south-eastern corner of the Terrace. It copies again the Tomb of Darius on the rocks of Naqsh-e Rostam (see no. 6.1). While his tomb is the only one bearing inscriptions at that site, this tomb on the slope of the mountain Rahmat at least names the representatives of the subject peoples that support the pedestal (*dais*). This tomb might have been the first one that was copied on the new site and, therefore, the necessity was felt to indicate the representations. If this assumption is correct, Artaxerxes II would have been the commissioner, if we follow the row of Achaemenid kings. A second hint is, that he was the last king to use three languages, Old Persian, Elamite and

152 / Apadana eastern stairway (left part), central scene on facade

Babylonian. Only inscriptions in Old Persian are preserved of his follower Artaxerxes III. There is a vestibule inside the tomb and just one tomb-chamber with two stone coffins, of which the first one is larger than the one behind it. They were covered with plano-convex lids.

4.23. The Unfinished Tomb

About 500 m south-east of the Terrace in a low spur of the mountain another royal tomb had been started but was never finished. It faces away from the Terrace. Only the upper register with the standing king in front of the altar and the Ahura Mazda symbol above it are executed, while the rest looks like a quarry. Two semi-finished guards on the left side wall give an interesting glimpse into the techniques of masons.

This tomb might have been prepared for the last Achaemenid king, Darius III (336/5-330 BC), who was defeated by Alexander the Great and was killed while flying away by his own satrap in the north-east of the empire.

153 / Water basin on the slope of Kuh-e Rahmat (next to no. 4.22)

154 / The Unfinished Tomb

155 / Persepolis, tomb of Artaxerxes II (Tomb V)

156 / Persepolis, general view of the tomb of Artaxerxes III

4.24. The Quarry in the North of the Terrace

On the way back to the entrance, before leaving, one should go from the Gate of all Lands a few steps to the north onto the walls. A quarry, in which the stones used on the Terrace were cut, can be seen from that spot. During building activities, presumably, a ramp for transporting stones led up to the Terrace. On the Terrace, next to the walls, an unfinished door-sill and a few steps further on an only roughly rounded column-drum are to be seen (fig. 9, D). The bosses around which the ropes for the transport could be fixed are still protruding.

5. Remains in the Neighbourhood of the Terrace of Persepolis

5.1. The Buildings at the Foot of the Terrace

While the representative and administrative centre lay on the Terrace of Persepolis, the city was situated in the plain. It must have been widely spread and was already known before the Terrace was built by Darius. But, only very few buildings have been excavated until now and nearly nothing has been published.

157 / The Rock-cistern

158 / The Buildings at the Foot of the Terrace

In the south of the Terrace remains of two palatial buildings have been excavated, but they have not yet been published. The excavator E.F. Schmidt has given a plan. There is an Apadana-like building in the centre with porticoes on three sides, except for the south, with two rows of four columns and towers at the corners. The main hall had four by four columns. An open courtyard in the east was bordered with stone walls crowned with crenelations. Stairs led to the yard, the level of which is 40-50 cm lower. At least one of the staircases was flanked by animal sculptures.

159 / A mortar of green chert

5.2. The so-called Fratadara-Temple (or Frataraka-Temple)

160 / Persepolis, gray limestone mastiff statue from south-eastern tower of the Apadana

A part of the city has been excavated to the north-west of the Terrace, but only a preliminary sketch-plan exists. This district is recognizable by an upright window-frame with reliefs on both sides. They are very much weathered and hardly discernible. They were much better preserved on the plates of Schmidt's publication. The figure on one side seems to wear the Iranian riding-costume with bashlyk and carries a bundle in his hands which has been identified as barsom. Such barsom-bundles were used by magi during their religious ceremonies for kindling the fire. This representation induced the excavator E. Herzfeld to assume that all the surrounding building-remains belonged to a fire-sanctuary. On the basis of former – uncorrect - reading of inscriptions on post-Achaemenid silver-coins, which were found in Persepolis, he attributed it to the assumed dynasty of Fratadara.

It has been shown that there are several buildings, which do not belong together, with a street in-between them. The most spectacular building opens to the street with a portico. Finely cut column-bases in the inner hall and a rectangular base with fine profiles in the middle of the back-wall have been preserved. It is still to be seen that something was fixed on its top, maybe a statue. A door led to smaller rooms which lay behind. The whole extent of the building is not known. Because of the former wrong connection of this building with the window-frame and its attribution to a fire-temple, this building is often referred to as an Achaemenid sanctuary, but there is nothing that could support such an assumption. Until now, we do not know anything about its function.

161 / Naqsh-e Rostam, the so-called Fire-altars at Hosain Kuh

5.3. The Takht-e Gohar or Takht-e Rostam

On the way to Naqsh-e Rostam, immediately after leaving the road running to Pasargadae, a large stone-base is to be seen in the fields to the left. It is composed of huge blocks. Obviously, something was to be built on it. It has been proposed that this might have been the foundation for a tomb like that one of Cyrus in Pasargadae (no. 10.1). If this assumption were correct it would have been destined for Cambyses, but was never finished, because he died so early on his way back from Egypt (see chapter 1.1).

5.4. The Palace in the Dasht-e Gohar

Some 150 m to the east of Takht-e Gohar (no. 5.3) remains of a large palatial building have been discovered, now covered again by fields.

162 / Naqsh-e Rostam, Reconstruction of the so-called Fire-altars at Hosain Kuh

Five bases of columns were found in situ. They consisted of square foundation slabs of grey limestone with neatly worked *tori* of light-coloured limestone on the top and belonged to a portico which used to have two rows with 14 columns each. The portico is situated in the north-east of the palatial building. Its estimated length is c. 55 m, its depth c. 9 m. The main hall of the building may have consisted of five rows of eight columns, of which several bases were found.

These bases were larger than those of the portico and the *tori* were cut from dark limestone. The columns itself may have been of wood because there is no trace of a special treatment with smoothed border and rougher picked inner circle *(anathyrosis)* on the *tori*, which would have been necessary, if stone-drums should have been added. Several foundation slabs of smaller size than in the main hall, found in the north of the building, suggest the existence of another portico to this side. The building has the same orientation as the so-called Takht-e Gohar. Thus, both structures may have belonged to the same plan. The smaller size of the portico-columns as well as the use of dark and light stone are comparable to the Palaces in Pasargadae (see no. 10.3 and 10.4). These facts show that the Palace had been built before the accession of Darius to the throne, who started his building activities on the Terrace of Persepolis.

6. Naqsh-e Rostam (fig. 163)

About 6 km to the north of Persepolis lies a rock-plateau, covered with reliefs, which slopes towards the south. It is locally called Naqsh-e Rostam which means "Plate of Rostam". Rostam is the most famous hero in the Iranian national epos, the Shahnameh, "Book of Kings". This place was chosen by King Darius for his burial-ground, and it must have been still in Sassanian times, especially, in the 3rd c., a much honoured site. In that time it was enclosed by a fortification wall with seven semicircular towers, which appear today as a mound of earth.

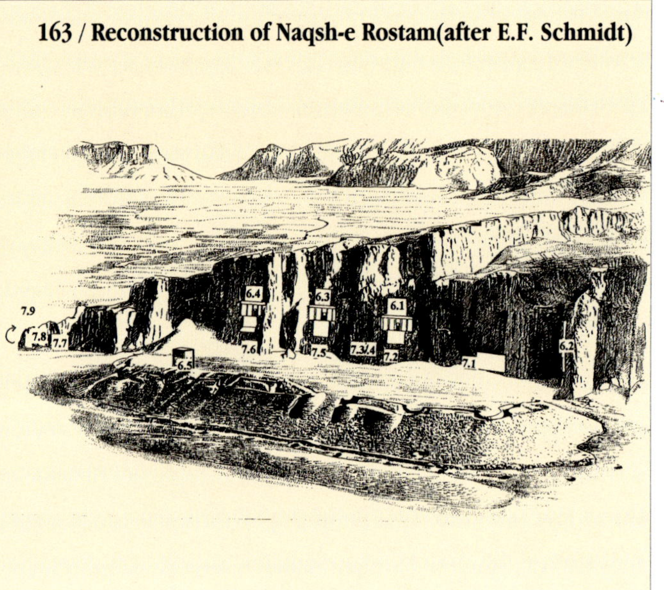

163 / Reconstruction of Naqsh-e Rostam(after E.F. Schmidt)

6.1. The Tomb of Darius the Great (522-486 BC, Tomb I) - 6.2. The Tomb of Xerxes (? 486-465 BC, Tomb II) - 6.3. The Tomb of Artaxerxes I (? 465-425/4 BC, Tomb III) - 6.4. The Tomb of Darius II (? 425/4-405/4 BC, Tomb IV) - 6.5. The so-called Ka'baye Zardosht - 7.1. The Relief of King Narseh (293-302 AD) - 7.2. The Double Relief of King Bahram I (273-276) and King Bahram II (276-293 AD) - 7.3. The Triumphal Relief of King Shapur I (241-272 AD) - 7.4. The Relief of the High-Priest Karder (c. 290 AD) - 7.6. The Relief of King Hormizd II (303-309 AD) - 7.6. The Relief of King Hormizd I (272-273 AD) - 7.7. The Relief of King Bahram II (276-293 AD) and the Elamite Relief - 7.8. The Relief of King Ardeshir I (224-241 AD) - 7.9. The so-called Fire-Altars at Hosain Kuh

*6.1. The Tomb of Darius the Great (522-486 BC, Tomb I)

With this kind of rock-cut tomb Darius created a new type for which prototypes are not known. The facade is cut into the rocks and forms a nearly 23 m high cross (cf. fig. 166). The middle part shows the facade of a building, upper and lower parts are 10,90 m wide. Let's look first at the relief in the middle. Four columns with bull-capitals support the entablature which is indicated by an architrave with three plain bands projecting in steps and dentils. Projecting walls (*antae*) are on both sides. The space between the columns was left blank without any indication of windows. The door

164 / Naqsh-e Rostam with the tombs of the first Achaemenid kings and Sassanian rock reliefs; on the right the so-called Ka'baye Zardosht

165 / Naqsh-e Rostam, the double relief of King Bahram I (273-276) and King Bahram II (276-293 AD) under the tomb of Darius the Great

in the middle leads into a corridor which is cut into the rocks parallel to the facade. One tomb-chamber lies exactly opposite the entrance-door, two more follow to the left side. Each contains three sarcophagi cut from the rocks. Only small fragments of the lids have been preserved, but that is enough to see that their form is different. Those in the chamber opposite the entrance were slightly rounded while the others were like a gabled roof. That might be a hint, that they were not all executed at the same time. The rounded lid-form occurs in all the other tombs of Darius' successors and also on early Achaemenid sarcophagi in the region of Sardes, the capital of the Lydian satrapy. So, the three sarcophagi opposite the entrance fit well into Achaemenid times. Therefore, the question is, if the other two chambers in Darius' tomb might have been added at another time, the date of which can not so easily be determined. It has been proposed that they might have been added as late as in Sassanian times (3rd c. AD).

The facade of the Tomb exactly reproduces the facade of the Palace of Darius in Persepolis (see no. 4.5). The measurements correspond to the cm. Though there are no windows indicated at the Tomb, the entrance-door has the same size as on the Palace (but the cornice shows 38 flutes, while the Palace door has only 26).

166 / Naqsh-e Rostam, general view of the tomb of Darius II (?)

167 / Naqsh-e Rostam, tomb of Artaxerxes I (?).

So, with the help of the Tomb-relief it is possible to reconstruct the former appearance of the Palace where the columns are now missing. The Palace in Persepolis can be considered as the "office" of the king. From there the whole empire was ruled. If the Tomb is reminiscence of this building it is also reminiscence of the deeds of the king. This idea is emphasized by a long inscription which is chiselled on the rocks between the columns. Here the king gives a report of his reign. The Old Persian version (DNb) is carved into the intercolumnium to the left of the door in the middle, the Elamite version to its right and the Babylonian on the easternmost panel. In Seleucid times an Aramaic inscription was added below the Elamite. The inscription is called "The Testament of King Darius", but – despite of its importance - it is too long and badly preserved to render it here in full size. Striking is the fact that the king emphasizes: *"Don't take that for the best, what somebody whispers into your ear; rather listen to that, what is said in public! You, young man, don't take that for excellent, what the mighty one is doing; what the meager one achieves, rather to that pay attention!"* And in a similar way the upper reliefs represent a political program, too. There the king (about 2,7 m high) stands on a throne-like pedestal, the legs of which are capped by lion-griffins. They are comparable to the capitals in the eastern Apadana

168 / Naqsh-e Rostam, general view of the tomb of Artaxerxes I (?).

portico. This throne is carried by representatives of all the subject peoples of the empire in two tiers, altogether 30. Thus, they demonstrate their support to the reign of the king. This program shows the same intention as that one of the Apadana-staircase (no. 4.3) where the peoples come to offer their gifts to the king. We can conclude that the Apadana, the Palace and the Tomb must have been planned at more or less the same time. And it would not have been possible to copy the facade of the Palace on the Tomb if it had not yet been, at least, planned. The king stands on a stepped base, holding his bow in the left hand and greeting with the right the symbol of the God Ahura Mazda who hovers over the whole scene (fig. 167). The god presents the "ring of power" to the king. An altar, on which fire is kindled as a symbol of worship of the god, stands on another second base in front of the king. (For the two bases and the altar see the Sacred Precinct in Pasargadae, no. 10.7). The upper right corner shows a disk with a crescent in its lower part, possibly, representing both, the sun and the moon.

Another long inscription, which names once more the peoples belonging to his empire, is in the back of the king (DNa). He emphasized that he got the power only by will and support of the God Ahura Mazda, he asked Ahura Mazda for further protection and warned everybody always to follow the orders of Ahura Mazda. To the left of the inscription –on the protruding left wall- three soldiers frame the scene. The topmost is identified by an inscription (DNc): "*Gaubarva (Greek Gobryas), a Patiskhorian, spear-bearer of Darius, the King*". Below him, with his own trilingual inscription (DNd), follows: "*Aspathines, clothes-bearer, holds the bow-case of Darius, the King*". Above his left shoulder appears this bow-case (gorytos). His dagger, suspended from the belt, is mostly destroyed. The guard on the bottom is not identified in any way. He must belong to the king's personal guards. More of them are depicted on the left side wall, two figures on top and one on the two panels below. Their pendants on the right side wall hold a fabric in front of their mouths, thus, presumably, indicating mourning. The succeeding Achaemenid kings copied this tomb-facade again and again, three times in Naqsh-e Rostam and then in Persepolis (see no. 4.19, 4.22, 4.23). None of these tombs bears an inscription which would attribute it to a certain king. So, we can only guess in which order they might have been executed. It is usually believed, that the Tomb of Xerxes might be to the right of the Tomb of Darius, on the rock looking to the west. The two tombs to the left are supposed to be of Artaxerxes I and Darius II.

169 / Naqsh-e Rostam, general view of the tomb of Xerxes (?).

6.2. The Tomb of Xerxes (? 486-465 BC, Tomb II)

This tomb lies about 100 m east-northeast of Darius' Tomb, facing westwards. It shows the best preserved reliefs. For their description confer (no. 6.1). Inside the tomb a vestibule and only one vault with three stone coffins are cut in the rock. This might suggest that also Darius' Tomb had originally just one vault. The lids of the sarcophagi show a flat bottom and a convex top.

6.3. The Tomb of Artaxerxes I (? 465-425/4 BC, Tomb III)

This tomb is located about 37 m west-southwest of Darius' Tomb. (For the description of the reliefs, see no. 6.1) . The inner vestibule is badly oriented so that it pierces the rock facade in its south-western corner. Three vaults are cut from the rocks, but only with one stone coffin each. The lid of the easternmost has been preserved. It shows a flat-bottomed rectangular slab curving upwards from each side.

6.4. The Tomb of Darius II (? 425/4-405/4 BC, Tomb IV)

This tomb lies about 33 m south-west of the preceding one (no. 6.3). Its facade and inner vaults are similar to the latter tomb, but they are more neatly spaced. All three lids of the stone coffins are preserved.

*6.5. The so-called Ka'baye Zardosht

One peculiar building stands in front of the rock-facade at a certain distance from the last tomb (no. 6.4). Today it is called Ka'baye Zardosht "the Ka'ba (cube) of Zoroaster". The ancient level was some meters deeper so that the building is now in a pit. But it gives an idea how much higher the reliefs of the whole site must have seemed to a visitor in ancient times. The tower-like building is copied after a similar one in Pasargadae (see no. 10.5). Their function has not yet been established. The plan is square (7,3 m) with projecting piers at the corners. Its height is 12,77 m and together with the flat pyramidal roof it reached 14,12 m high. Three pairs of false windows in dark stone give the impression of three stories. All four facades are ornamented in an unusual way with uniformly staggered rectangular depressions. They might refer to something special which cannot be determined until now. Steep stairs lead to the only door which is high above the ground-level. The door (originally 1,75 m high) may have been of stone. It locked the room inside (3,72 by 3,74 m, 5,54 m high). It has been proposed that it might have been a tomb. But in this case

the question remains for whom it was intended. Others thought it was a fire-temple. But how to keep a fire in that high up room without any windows? In Sassanian times king Shapur I (241-272) added a large inscription covering the lower parts of the building which had originally been left blank. Like the Achaemenid inscriptions it is given in three languages, but this time in Middle Persian (Pahlavi; eastern side), Parthian (western side) and Greek (southern side). There, he records all his deeds, military as well as religious. This inscription is, therefore, of high importance. Towards the end of the century Kartir, the head of the Zoroastrian state-church and an extremely powerful man, added an inscription of his own (which is similar to that one on the reliefs, no. 7.4 and 8.2) below the Middle Persian version on the east side. But, here he mentions the building on which the inscriptions are written, calling it ***bun-chanak***, "foundation-house". The holy script of the Avesta, the bible of the Zoroastrians, is also called "foundation". Therefore, the holy script of the Avesta might have been kept in this house.

171 / Naqsh-e Rostam, tomb of Xerxes; King, god, and fire-altar in the top register

7. Sassanian Reliefs in Naqsh-e Rostam (fig. 163)

This site with the Achaemenid royal tombs was still honoured in Sassanian times by the Sassanian kings. After defeating the Parthian kings who had the power over Iran for centuries (3rd c. BC - 3rd c. AD), the Sassanians tried to legitimate their reign by tracing back their line to the Achaemenids. Thus, the site of the tombs of their "ancestors" must have had a special meaning for them. And even more, their capital Istakhr (see under chapter 9) lay just a few hundred meters away from this place. So, during the 3rd c. AD several reliefs were added to the old tomb-facades.

7.1. The Relief of King Narseh (293-302 AD)

The relief to the right of the Tomb of Darius is the last one that was executed on this site. There is no inscription but the king's crown makes identification possible. Every Sassanian ruler had his personal crown. Those crowns are well known from the coins. The relief shows the investure of King Narseh, the youngest son of Shapur I, through the goddess Anahita, who is standing to the right. She offers the king the

172 / Naqsh-e Rostam, relief depicting the investiture of Narseh by Anahita

"ring of power" as in former times god Ahura Mazda did to Darius. This is the only example that the investure is done by Anahita. The other reliefs of the early Sassanian kings always show Ahura Mazda in this function. A smaller figure, dressed in the same way as the king, stands between the king and the goddess. This may be the crown-prince. A man with a peculiar cap which must indicate his rank follows behind the king. He raises his hand with a bent and pointing finger, a typical Sassanian gesture indicating reference to a superior. The relief is not finished to the left. There should have followed another man whose picture has never been fully executed. To the right of this relief a large rectangular space has been provided, but no relief is to be seen. A dating is therefore impossible.

7.2. The Double Relief of King Bahram I (273-276) and King Bahram II (276-293 AD)

There is a double-relief cut into the rocks under the facade of the Tomb of Darius the Great (no. 6.1). Both representations, one above the other, show an encounter of two horsemen. The victorious one is coming from the left. The king in the upper relief is recognizable by his crown. He is Bahram II. This relief reaches into the upper parts of the lower one, which, therefore, seems to be older. It might have belonged to his father Bahram I. In both representations the adversary, who already stumbles to the ground together with his horse, is not characterized by any detail. Therefore, he cannot be named in either case. On both reliefs a knight holding the standard is standing behind the ruler. The motif is copied from the, presumably, earliest Sassanian relief near Firuzabad, which shows Ardeshir defeating the last Parthian king Artaban V (213-224).

7.3. The Triumphal Relief of King Shapur I (241-272 AD)

A monumental relief showing the triumph of king Shapur I over two Roman emperors is to the left of the Tomb of Darius. The king, over life-size, can be identified by his crown with the large bunch which reaches higher than the upper border of the relief. Shapur, who is on horseback, turns to the left and grasps with his right hand the right hand of a standing Roman emperor. A second emperor went respectfully down on his knees before the king. These two must be the Roman emperors Philippus Arabs, with whom he signed a peace-treaty in 244, and Valerian, whom Shapur imprisoned in 260 AD. But until now the discussion continues about the correct identification of each of the two figures on the relief.

7.4. The Relief of the High-Priest Kartir (c. 290 AD)

A portrait and a long inscription of the highest magus of the state, Kartir, is in the back of King Shapur combined with his relief (no. 7.3). The high-priest wears a necklace of big pearls and a high cap with the symbol of scissors on it. This symbol might refer to his name, which could mean "the cutter". He raises his hand with the gesture of worship towards the image of the king. But he added his own relief only when king Shapur was already dead for many years. This we can say not only because of the fact, that it would not have been appropriate to join one's relief with that of the king, but also because of his inscription, in which Kartir describes his career and increasing power. Under Shapur he had not yet had such a high rank. He served seven Sassanian kings altogether. A shorter version of this inscription appears on the Ka'baye Zardosht (no. 6.5) and a synopsis in Naqsh-e Rajab (see no. 8.2).

7.6. The Relief of King Hormizd II (303-309 AD)

Another relief with the representation of an encounter of two horsemen, comparable to no. 7.2, is at the foot of the Achaemenid Tomb III (no. 6.3). Again the king can be identified by his crown. It is winged and above the forehead shaped as a bird's head holding a spherical bead in its beak. Therefore, it must be the crown of Hormizd II.

The remains of another relief are on the top of this relief, somewhat shifted to the right. It is badly weathered and, therefore, it is not possible to reconstruct its former representation.

7.7. The Relief of King Hormizd I (272-273 AD)

Like the preceding relief and (no. 7.2) a fight on horseback is rendered here, too. But this time, the opponent rider is still on horseback, attacking his adversary. Just the direction from which the king is coming and the fact, that he and his horse are in the foreground, overlapping the other figures, indicate the winner. The king wears a peculiar crown with wide protruding tips, forward and backward, and a ball in the middle. In addition he has a ball on each shoulder. These were, presumably, made of metal and thus glittered in the sun. Shapur I is wearing the same balls on Ardeshir's relief in Firuzabad. At that time Shapur had been still crown prince. On the basis of comparison this relief in Naqsh-e Rostam may be attributed to Hormizd I, the son of Shapur and his daughter Adhar-Anahid, who reigned only few months.

173 / Naqsh-e Rostam, relief showing the triumph of Shapur I over Valerian, bust and inscription of Kartir at the right end

Following the way at the foot of the mountain to the west one passes several smaller cuttings into the rocks, rectangular panels, which have only been prepared, but no relief had been executed.

7.8. The Relief of King Bahram II (276-293 AD) and the Elamite Relief

The king, recognizable by his winged crown, stands upright in the middle. To his right follow members of his family, presumably his two sons and his wife. High ranked nobles as indicated by their caps are standing to his left. But their identification is not sure. The high-priest Kartir with the symbol of scissors on his cap is represented on the left end of the relief, that is, on the side of the family. Kartir's symbol appears again in the upper left corner of the relief and might signify that it was him who ordered this relief to honour the King Bahram II.

The shape of the relief is quite unusual. Only the king is rendered in full size. The other persons are only to be seen to their waists. And around the corner of the rock, on the right, there is another figure which looks quite different in size and execution. It has a rounded cap with a point above the forehead. This cap was fashioned in Elamite in the second half of the 2nd mill. BC. Thus, this figure belongs to a much

174 / Naqsh-e Rostam, relief showing the investure of Ardeshir I by god Ahura Mazda

175 / Naqsh-e Rostam, Sassanian relief attributed to Hormizd I, equestrian combat

older relief, the oldest one that had been executed on this site (presumably 12th c. BC). Only few parts of the former relief are still recognizable: under the nobles of Bahram II on the right side there are traces of two Elamite snake-thrones. They had served as seats for two gods, presumably, a couple. On the left side a small figure wearing a crenelated crown can be identified. This might be a later addition to the Elamite relief (9th c. BC?).

176 / Naqsh-e Rostam, relief depicting the equestrian combat of King Hormizd II

7.9. The Relief of King Ardeshir I (224-241 AD)

At the very end of this mountain-site is a beautiful relief which has still preserved large parts of its finely polished surface. It shows the investure of King Ardeshir by god Ahura Mazda. Both are on horseback. The god is given in Sassanian attire with a huge bunch of curls on his head and others falling on his shoulders. He offers the king the "ring of power". Under the feet of his horse the defeated Ahriman, the evil, is lying. The king approaches the god with the gesture of worship. His hair forms a high bunch on his head, covered with a fine cloth. The defeated Artaban V, the last Parthian king, is to be seen under the feet of his horse. He is recognizable by the emblem on his cap. Both horses bear an inscription in Middle Persian, Parthian and Greek, indicating the person who is represented. Ardeshir's inscription reads: *"This is the picture of his Zoroastrian majesty Ardeshir, King of Kings of Iran, whose decent is from the gods, son of his majesty, King Papak."*

7.10. The so-called Fire-Altars at Hosain Kuh

Next to the relief of King Ardeshir (no. 7.9) the rocks turn sharply to the north. Following the road which leads along the foot of the mountain, one passes an ancient quarry. Some steps further two stone monuments are visible. They are cut from the rocks together with the base. Both are adorned with arcades on all four sides and protruding columns at the corners. Around the upper borders are egg-shaped crenelations. Both have a bowl-like depression at their top. These monuments are usually regarded as fire-altars. But in comparison with monuments which are preserved in other regions it is more likely that these were Sassanian graves. Only the bones were gathered and kept in the depression at the top. Originally they were covered by cap-like lids, which in this case have not been preserved.

177 / Naqsh-e Rostam, relief depicting Bahram II and his court, carved over a Pre-Achaemenid relief

178 / General view of Naqsh-e Rajab, (Flandin and Coste, La Perse ancienne)

8. Naqsh-e Rajab

Another important Sassanian site, hidden behind small rocks, lies at the spot in which the street going to Naqsh-e Rostam departs from the main-road Persepolis-Pasargadae (fig. 2). This might have already been a place of worship in very early times. Then, it was chosen by Ardeshir I (224-241 AD) for his investure-relief and others followed. The description starts with the relief on the left side and continues to the right.

8.1. The Relief of King Shapur I (241-272 AD) and his Court

The largest and most impressive relief of this site is the one on the left. It shows the king - emphasized by size - on horseback. Unfortunately, his face has been destroyed. But his dress is beautifully cut and his horse richly adorned. The nobles of the court are standing behind the king. The last ones are reduced to just the upper parts of their bodies because the rock slopes down on that side. Three men directly behind the king are shown with special emblems on their caps. But we know only one of them and that is worn by the nobleman in front who stands there in full representation,

179 / Naqsh-e Rajab, King shapur I and his Court

not overlapped by any other person. Such rendering already stresses his importance. His emblem is the same as that of crown-prince Shapur on the large relief near Firuzabad showing the defeat of the Parthian king Artaban V by Ardeshir, the first Sassanian king. So, we should assume that this person must be Shapur himself. The inscription on the breast of the horse and on the background in front of it names Shapur as king. But, how could he be rendered twice? Evidently, this is a very strange place for the inscription. And on the large free space in front of the king there are clearly discernible traces of another inscription which has been chiselled away. So, we can only assume that there were alterations. The most possible solution is that the relief had been made by Ardeshir and then reworked by Shapur who erased the inscription of his father and added his own. This relief and the one showing the investure of Ardeshir in Naqsh-e Rostam (see no. 7.4) are the only reliefs with such a fine polishing of the surface.

8.2. The Relief of the High-Priest Kartir

The portrait of Kartir, comparable to that one in Naqsh-e Rostam is to the left of the Ardeshir-relief (no. 8.3). Again he is clearly identified by the scissors on his cap. The inscription is a summery of that one in Naqsh-e Rostam.

8.3. The Investure of King Ardeshir I (224-241 AD)

This must have been the earliest relief on this site. The figures are very straight and stiff. The main figures are the king and the god Ahura Mazda. The former is looking towards the latter who offers him the "ring of power". In this case both are standing. Below their hands is a small scene with two figures. One is nude and carries a club, thus obviously represents Heracles. So, we may assume that the other small person is Bahram, the oldest son of Shapur and the grandson of Ardeshir, because his name Bahram is the Iranian equivalent of Heracles. Crown-prince Shapur is, presumably, to be recognized in the bearded man on the left. The rock-surface is so much destroyed that it is impossible to discern if there was his emblem on the cap. To the right, separated by a post, are two more figures; one is wearing a peculiar cap ending in an animal-head. These might be the wives of the king and the crown-prince. They turn away from the main scene thus indicating that they had to stay in the house and were not participating in an official act.

8.4. The Investure of King Shapur I (241-272 AD)

The last relief, on the right nearly disappearing in the rocks, shows the investure of Shapur by the god Ahura Mazda, both on horse-back. They are similarly clad, the god with big bunches of curls according to the Sassanian fashion. This relief is created after the prototype of Ardeshir's investure in Naqsh-e Rostam (no. 7.8), but without accompanying figures.

9. Istakhr

On the way from Persepolis to Pasargadae after circa 7 km one passes the ancient site of Istakhr (fig. 181), the first capital of the Sassanian empire. In this city the founder of the new dynasty, Sasan, was local ruler and high-priest at the sanctuary of Anahita. To the left of the street a mound of earth indicates the location of the old town. To the right there are remains of a gate.

9.1. The Takht-e Tavous

Huge stone-blocks of the gate, which have been preserved, are today called Takht-e Tavous, "peacock-throne". The structure has not yet been studied in detail and there have not been any excavations though it would be of high interest. The gate seems to be combined with water-canals. They bring water from the nearby mountain, and the canal continues to Naqsh-e Rajab and from there to Persepolis. It has been proposed that the structure might be Sassanian but the water-canal would have been of more importance in Achaemenid times.

9.2. The Building in Istakhr (so-called Old Mosque) (fig. 182)

Very little investigation was undertaken inside the former walls. Ruins of a large building clearly show Achaemenid features. It has been identified as the Old Mosque, for which Achaemenid columns were reused. Fine examples of bases and addorsed-bull capitals are visible. But there are also remains of massive walls and door-jambs. It is hardly possible that they were removed from another place. Therefore, it seems to be an Achaemenid palatial building on its original place. This would confirm that already in Achaemenid times there must have been a palace or a settlement on this place.

180 / Naqsh-e Rajab, relief of Kartir

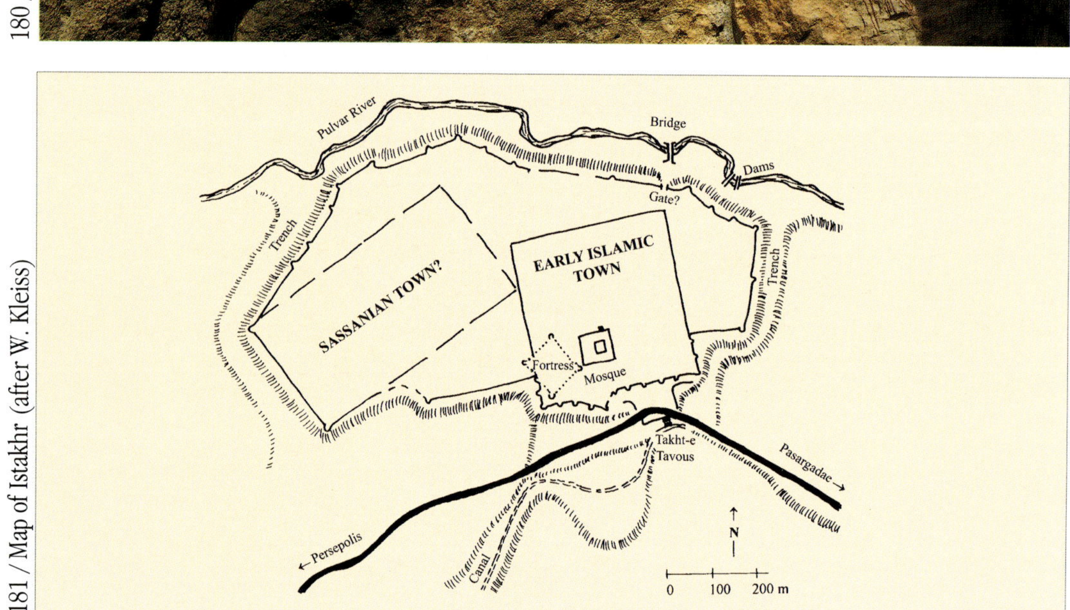

181 / Map of Istakhr (after W. Kleiss)

182 / Achaemenid remains of Istakhr

9.3. The Remains of a Sassanian Building

About 200 m from the Achaemenid building there are scattered architectonical pieces of a Sassanian building with architraves and shell-like niches. Between those fragments is a neatly cut stone-block with relief on one side. It depicts left hand and thigh of a female figure (now behind the museum in Persepolis).
It compares well with the rendering of the goddess Anahita on King Narseh's relief in Naqsh-e Rostam (no. 7.1). So this stone-block might be extremely important. It proves that relief did exist on buildings, too. And with its representation it could have been even part of the famous sanctuary of Anahita in Istakhr.

10. Pasargadae

In 555 BC the Persian King Cyrus, who was later called "the Great", defeated the Median forces and laid the foundations of the Persian Empire (see chapter 1.1). The decisive battle took place near the fortress Pasargadae and in this area Cyrus built his new capital. Pasargadae is situated in the Morghab-Valley, through which the main road from Shiraz to Isfahan passes. Because of the importance of this site and its strong connections to Persepolis, for which it functioned as the prototype, a short survey of the most important monuments is given here (fig. 185).

183 / Pasargadae, fanciful reconstruction by Madame Dieulafoy

10.1. The Tomb of Cyrus the Great (559-530BC)

An avenue lined by trees on both sides leads directly to the Tomb of King Cyrus. It is a free standing monument of massive stonework. The building is raised on a base of six receding tiers, of which the lowest is 1,65 m high. The original height of the monument must have been c. 11,10 m. The Tomb looks like a small house with gabled roof, measuring 6,40 by 5,35 m. The inner chamber is 3,17 m in length, while the width and height are 2,11 m. The sarcophagus of King Cyrus, allegedly made

184 / Pasargadae, tomb of Cyrus the Great

of gold, once stood in this chamber. It is more likely, that it was gilded bronze. Another hollow compartment above the chamber in the roof may have been executed for structural reasons.

There are no prototypes for this type of building which is, despite of its simplicity, still very impressive. Cyrus might have seen similar tombs on his campaign to Lydia against the famous and fabulously rich king Croisus. But there, the tombs were totally covered by hills of earth, while the idea of raising it up on a high plinth might have been Cyrus' own.

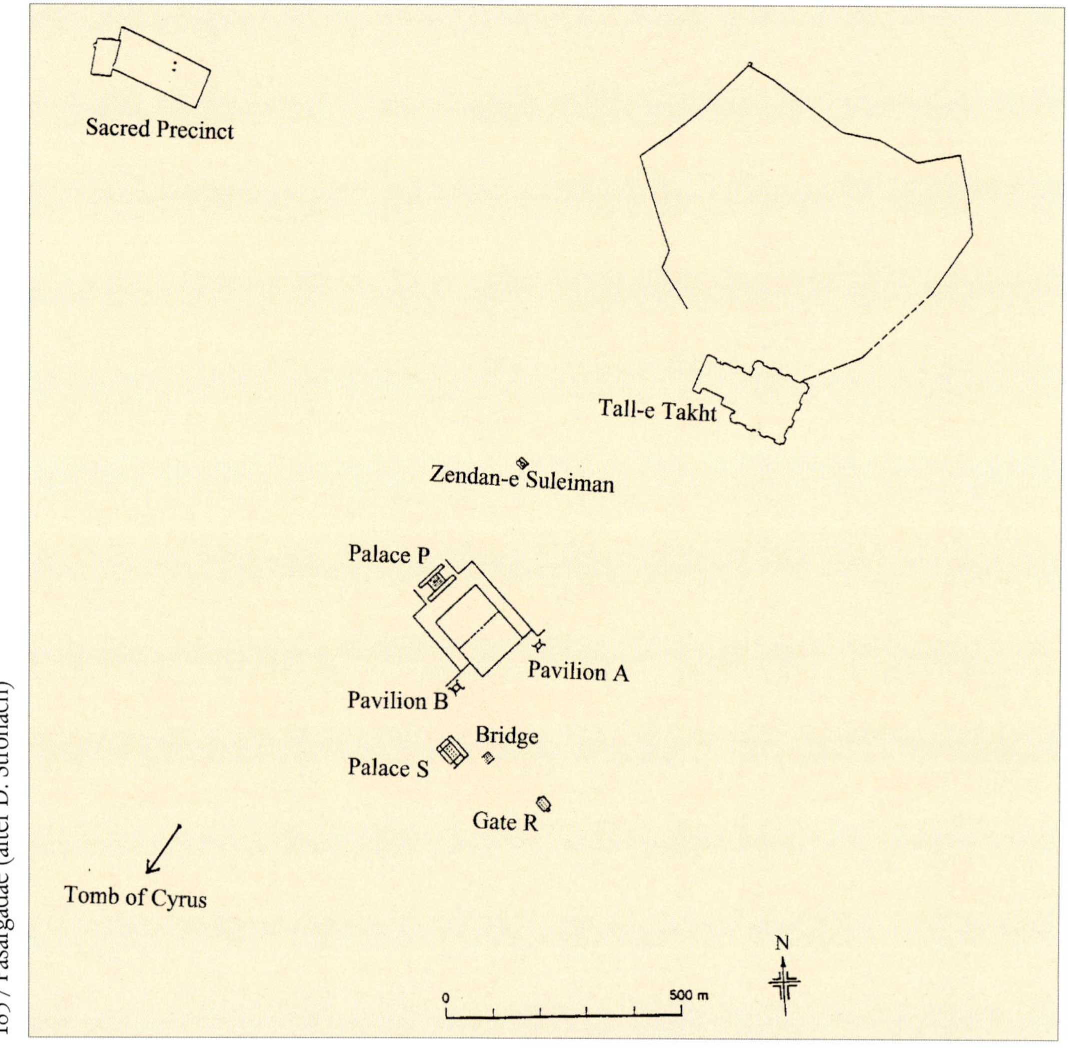

185 / Pasargadae (after D. Stronach)

10.2. The Gate with Relief (Gate R) (fig. 187)

The buildings in the plain of Pasargadae were arranged according to a masterful plan. A large palace-precinct with two palaces (no. 10.3 and 10.4), pavillons, gardens and water-canals was in the centre. The access to this area was provided by a rectangular gate-building (28,50 by 25,50 m). Two rows of four columns each once supported the roof. The south-eastern entrance and the one on the opposite site were emphasized by their size and the use of dark stones. Large bull-sculptures were guarding both doors. Tiny fragments of these sculptures, which had been found during early excavations but later disappeared, and comparable measurements of the building suggest, that the entrance-gate of Persepolis was modelled after this prototype.

186 / Pasargadae, the jambs of the south-eastern door showing a genius with fish-cloak, followed by a rampant bull

Two much smaller doorways of white stone pierced the long walls in their middle. Only one jamb of the north-eastern door has been preserved. It bears the famous representation of a four-winged figure (see the copy in the Persepolis Museum, no. 4.11), which turns towards the centre of the building. The bearded figure wears a long fringed dress with rosette-borders which is known as a garment of Elamite princes. An impressive Egyptian crown, mounted on a close fitting cap, is rendered on its head. The meaning of this figure is much contested. Some scholars have seen in it a picture of Cyrus himself, because originally an inscription was on top of the relief: *"I, Cyrus, the King, an Achaemenid"*. It might have been added by Darius (cf. no. 10.3) and has disappeared since more than 100 years. Thus, it is more likely, that on the relief a genius is represented, well known from Assyrian art, who protects the building and in this case has typical attributes of various regions of the Persian empire.

10.3. The Palace S (Audience Hall)

The Letter S stands for "Säule", meaning "Palace with the Column", referring to the only one column, which is still upright. The central hall (32,35 by 22,14 m) had two rows of four columns each. The slim white stone column (c. 13,10 m high) is standing on a stepped square base and a torus, altogether hewn from one piece of black stone. Only small fragments of the capitals have been found. They show four different types of animals: horned and crested lions (comparable to the capitals of the eastern Apadana portico, no. 4.3), lions, bulls and horses. It is the only instance of horses as capitals. All these fragments were again of black stone. The alternating use of white and black stone is to be seen in the entire building. Four doorways of black stone in the middle of each wall lead into the porticoes, which surrounded the building on all four sides.

The door-jambs were adorned with reliefs, the best preserved rests of which are to be seen in the north-western and south-eastern doorways. In each case a human figure is followed by a monster. From Assyrian parallels we know, that the north-western doorway once rendered a warrior with short skirt and horned cap and behind him a lion-demon with a dagger in one hand and a mace in the other. The jambs of the south-eastern door showed a genius with fish-cloak, followed by a rampant bull, holding a disc-topped standard. All figures looked towards the interior hall.

187 / Pasargadae, a jamb of the north-eastern door which bears the famous relief of the four-winged figure

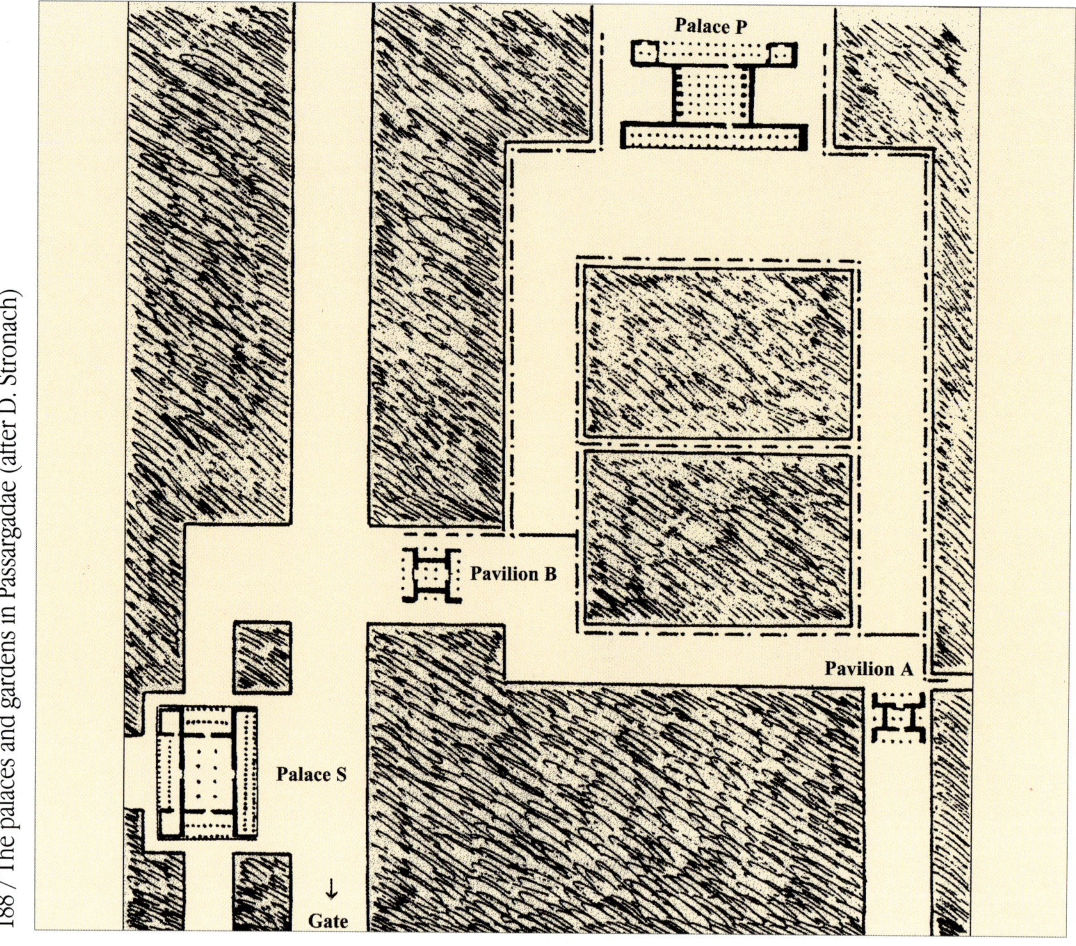

188 / The palaces and gardens in Passargadae (after D. Stronach)

From the eight corner pillars which once flanked the porticoes only one from the south-eastern portico has been preserved high enough to show the inscription in its upper part: *"I, Cyrus, the King, an Achaemenid."* This inscription must have been added by Darius, who wanted to legitimate his rule by pointing out, that Cyrus had been from the same family. Cyrus himself cannot have written the inscription because at his time the Persian script had not yet been invented.

The porticoes were of different size (see fig. 188) and were not half so high as the building. This is a decisive difference in relation to the buildings in Persepolis. The largest portico, which covered the entire width of the building, lay in the south-east and was directed towards the gardens.

10.4. The Palace P (Residential Palace)

At more than 300 m distance from Palace S lies the Palace P (fig. 188). Its name is derived from "Palast mit Pfeiler" = "Palace with pillar", because only one pillar was visible of the entire building, when excavations started almost 70 years ago. The pillar shows the same inscription as that one of Palace S (no. 10.3).
The plan of the building consists of a central hall (31,10 by 22,10 m) with five rows of six columns. Especially fine are the horizontally fluted *tori* of these white stone-columns. Striking is the fact, that all preserved drums were of the same height and no fragments of other drums have been found. This suggests, that they were never finished in stone. Indeed, fragments of plaster with ornaments in bright colours have been found. They show strong relations to the remnants of the wooden columns of the Treasury in Persepolis (no. 4.13). In addition five mud-brick piers have been supporting the roof at each end of the hall. A long portico (72,50 m long, 9,35 m deep) with two rows of 20 columns looks towards the gardens. A white stone-bench, once covered with a layer of black stone slabs, runs along the walls of the portico. At the mid-point a white stone-block projects. This may have been the place for the king's throne. A low stone block in front of it may have been the support for a footstool. Because of this central throne-place the door leading from the portico into the main hall and that one on the opposite site were shifted from the usual position to the side. The jambs of these two doors were adorned with reliefs, which are only partly preserved. They all showed the king, followed by an attendant, leaving the building. The garment of the king was richly adorned with metal-, probably gold-ornaments. A trilingual inscription, in Old-Persian, Elamite and Babylonian: *"Cyrus, the Great King, an Achaemenid"*, appeared on the folds. These reliefs are very close to those in the Palace of Darius in Persepolis (no. 4.5). It seems that this building was only begun by Cyrus and finished by Darius.

10.5. The Zendan-e Suleiman

At the northern edge of the Palace area are the remains of a stone tower which is called "Zendan-e Suleiman", "Prison of Solomon", by the local people. This was the prototype after which the Ka'baye Zardosht in Naqsh-e Rostam (no. 6.5) had been copied. For description and discussion of its function see there.

190 / Pasargadae, remains of the so-called Zendan-e Suleiman

191 / Pasargadae, the Tall-e Takht

189 / Pasargadae, Palaces

192 /A view of the ruins of Palace P in Pasargadae

10.6. The Tall-e Takht

While the palaces and gardens are situated in the plain another part of the capital of Cyrus was built on a rather steep hill, which the local people call "Takht-e Madar-e Suleiman", "Throne of the Mother of Solomon", or just "Tall-e Takht", "Throne-Hill". For hundreds of years after its construction this hill has been used as fortification. Cyrus had built a strong wall as substruction in the west of the platform. Still today one is impressed by the beauty of its stonework. It was the first structure of its kind in the whole Near East, presumably executed by Greek stonemasons. Over 70 masons' marks are reminiscent of the workers who once cut the stones. An inner wall of rough sandstone blocks was encased by perfectly dressed stone blocks which were jointed to each other without any mortar. Some of the horizontal layers were secured by iron clamps. They were the reason that in later times pilferers destroyed the facade in search of iron, which they wanted to reuse. Therefore, one can see the holes all over the wall. A staircase in the north gave access to the platform, clearly demonstrating, that in the time of its erection the terrace had not been fortified. A second staircase at some distance from the first was never finished. Nothing is left of the buildings which once stood on the platform. We can only imagine that here the administration of the early Achaemenid Empire might have been housed.

10.7. The Sacred Precinct

The Sacred Precinct lies isolated in the north-western corner of Pasargadae, but with the direct view to the Tomb of Cyrus in the distance. Only two large white stone plinths, set on durable foundations, are visible today. One of them (2,16 m high and 2,43 m square at the base) is connected with a staircase block. A band of highly polished black stone slabs with protruding corner slabs was laid around this assembly. Black stones might have embellished the upper part of the plinth, too. The second plinth (2,10 m high, 2,80 m square) stands at some distance to the north. It might have been topped by a fire-altar. Fragments of stepped altars, one with a deep fire-bowl, have been found scattered in Pasargadae. Accordingly an installation comparable to those which are rendered on the tomb-reliefs of the Achaemenid kings (fig. 167) must have existed here. The king could step up on the base with the stairs. The protruding slabs on the corners may have served as supports for a canopy. The altar with the fire stood at some distance before him. There are no remains of any buildings. That means, that in early Achaemenid times the fire had always to be rekindled before a ceremony.

193 / Two blocks of white stone belonging to the Sacred Precinct at Pasargadae

These plinths together with a wide space were enclosed by a wall of dry stone, which ends at the bottom of a mound. This mound once was shaped into five terraces by means of stone-walls. A carefully built mud-brick platform (15 by 20 m) was at its summit, while the third platform – and, maybe, others originally too – were paved with stones. It cannot be determined whether these platforms were constructed for visitors, who could pursue religious ceremonies from distance, or if other ceremonies took place here.

11. Objects from Persepolis in the National Museum in Tehran

Many of the most important finds from Persepolis are exhibited in the National Museum. Some of them shall be mentioned here in an appendix to complete the overall picture of Persepolis. The exhibition-halls on the groundfloor are arranged around two open courtyards, which supply daylight. The objects from Persepolis are exposed at the end of the right rectangular hall, in the smaller passage-hall leading to the left hall and in about one half of the latter one.

11.1. The largest object is the so-called Treasury Relief, which once adorned the central part of the northern staircase of the Apadana (no. 4.3). It is a mirror-view copy of the relief from the eastern staircase which is still in Persepolis (no. 4.14). This one is better preserved and gives, therefore, an idea of the former appearance of its pendant. Due to the mirror-view the figures are here depicted from the other side, so that the weapons of the king can be seen. The scabbard and the battle-axe are extremely finely executed.

11.2. Next to the "Treasury Relief" stands the stone-statue of Darius in a niche. It was made in Egypt and found at the entrance-building of his Palace in Susa. Unfortunately, the head is missing. This statue gives an impression of sculpture in the round, which once must have adorned the buildings on the Terrace of Persepolis, too. The king is wearing the Achaemenid court-dress with long, wide sleeves. His dagger is stuck into his girdle. An inscription in Old Persian, Elamite and Babylonian is written on the folds on the left side of the dress: "*The Great God is Ahura Mazda, who created this earth, who created yonder sky, who created man, who created happiness for man, who made Darius king. This is the statue of stone, which Darius the King ordered to be made in Egypt, that the man, who will be later, may see it and may know that the Persian man hold Egypt. I am Darius the Great King, King of Kings, King of lands,*

194 / Persepolis, bronze pedestal of three lions, found in the Treasury

King on this great earth, King Hystaspes' son, an Achaemenid. Saith Darius the King: Me may Ahura Mazda protect and all, what was made by me!" The girdle as well as the folds on the right side and the base are inscribed with Egyptian hieroglyphs. These inscriptions use the Egyptian formulas of royalty, calling Darius even a god. The long sides of the base show representations of the subject peoples in Egyptian style. –Reproductions of glazed tile-ornaments from the Palace of Darius in Susa adorn the walls of the niche.

11.3. The southern stairway of the Tripylon (no. 4.10) and one unit of its sphinx-capitals, all made of dark stone, have been restored on the other side of the niche.

11.4. Several cases with finds from the Treasury (no. 4.13) are on show in the passage hall in front of the above mentioned objects:

A masterly worked lion pedestal of bronze, which is cast in one piece, is to be seen opposite Darius' statue. Each lion is solidly attached to two other animals at flank and shoulder. A bar connects each lion with the cylindrical socket, the top of which is broken and bent outward. Deep gashes are to be seen along the back, on the back of the neck, down the back of each leg and across the top of each hind leg.

They might be either casting marks or something had been fixed in them. The function of this object is not yet determined, it may have been the base of a table. A tiny but interesting fragment is made of reddish stone showing the left hand of a man grasping the mane of a lion (cf. the reliefs with the royal hero, for instance in the Palace of Darius [no. 4.5] or in the Hall of 100 Columns [no. 4.15]). It is not sure, if this little sculpture was a statuette or belonged to a vessel. Several metal ornaments and inlay work have been found. Unique is a pair of bronze horses, cast in one piece. It was found in the portico of the Hall of 100 Columns (no. 4.15) and may have been part of a chariot scene in a frieze. It could have been attached to a wooden door or furniture.

Nearly 300 objects of green chert have been found in the Treasury, most of them were shattered into pieces and scattered on the floor. Mortars and pestles as well as plates and trays were made of this hard green stone, smoothed and then highly polished. They are inscribed with ink in Aramaic. From these inscriptions we learn, that the pieces were sent as tribute from the province of Arachosia. The mortars (cf. fig. 159) and pestles, presumably, served to prepare the haoma-drug. Unusual is a bowl with three lion legs.

11.5. Some fine examples of sculptures in the round are exhibited in front of the Tripylon staircase (no. 11.3).

The statue of a dog (fig. 160; head restored) has been found in the vestibule of the south-eastern tower of the Apadana (no. 4.3). The statue and pedestal were wrought from one piece of rock and then polished. Presumably, it can be determined as a mastiff. By its side was found the pedestal of a second, presumably identical dog, only its paws and parts of the hind legs have been preserved.

Two identical polished statues of couchant felines, perhaps leopards (only one is exhibited), were found in a palatial building. Base and animal were made from the same block of grey limestone. Though the head is missing, this sculpture appeals to the visitor, because of the lively rendering of the animals' features .

The upper part of a column together with its well preserved capital with addorsed bulls .

An unique find is to be seen on the opposite side of the room: a Greek marble statue of Penelope, the wife of Odysseus. This is the earliest preserved example (2nd half of 5th c. BC) of many later copies. The type must have been widely adored among the Greeks. The Achaemenid kings, who might have received this statue as

195 / The head of an Achaemenian woman or prince, made of lapis lazuli

a gift, kept it in their Treasury (no. 4.13).

11.6. Fragments of more than 600 vessels of royal tableware have been found shattered in the Treasury (no. 4.13). Presumably they were once set in precious metal or with gold overlay and therefore destroyed by the pilferers. Egyptian objects show inscriptions of rulers of the 26th dynasty, which ended with the Persian conquest. Of the Achaemenid rulers only the name of Xerxes is engraved on vessels. Some of the most spectacular pieces are on exhibition, distributed in several show-cases: Exceptional is a bottle-shaped vessel of blue composition (67,5 cm), the largest of all objects made of this material.

A granite bowl bears an inscription: *"Palace of Ashurbanipal, Great King, [Mighty King, King] of Totality, King of Assyria"* (668-627 BC). Four handles are shaped as lions, which appear to cling to the shoulder of the vessel. Between the lions strips of gold may have been applied, as pairs of holes at the sides of each animal suggest. The lions themselves were probably covered with gold, too, which had been fixed in depressions at both sides of their chests. Two small holes in the forehead of each lion and the eyes had once been inlaid.

Most elaborate is a granite bowl on high stalk, inscribed with Xerxes' name. Twelve swans seem to hold the bowl in their beaks (fig. 196).

Two heads and necks of swans form the handles of a tray. A palmette is set between their joined necks.

11.8. Besides all other scattered finds several hundred assorted units of lapis lazuli, carnelian, agate, onyx, sardonyx and rivets of gold, were found hidden in a hole in

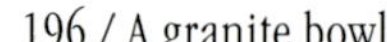

196 / A granite bowl

197 / Two curls of Lapis Lazulis Lazuli

a corner of the Treasury (no. 4.13). Lapis lazuli was especially high valued by the Achaemenids and some fine works of art are made of this material: The front part of a lion with wide open mouth is executed in all details. Especially the face shows a great agitation and liveliness.

A small head with crenelated crown may be one of rarely preserved examples of representation of a woman (if not of a beardless young man, fig 195).

The valuable lapis lazuli was often imitated by the so-called Egyptian blue (or blue composition), a special kind of faience. Several pieces of inlay and large curls in this material (fig. 197) are to be seen in show-cases. Some wall pegs are bearing a trilingual inscription, which amazingly establishes: *"Peg of 'lapis lazuli', made in the house of King Darius"*. They were found in Xerxes' Harem (no. 4.11), but their purpose has not yet been determined.